Encyclopedia of the Animal World

BIRDS

The Waterbirds

Robin Kerrod

WITH CONTRIBUTIONS BY

Jill Bailey

Facts On File
New York • Oxford

THE WATERBIRDS
The Encyclopedia of the Animal World:
Birds

Managing Editor: Lionel Bender
Art Editor: Ben White
Designer: Malcolm Smythe
Text Editor: Miles Litvinoff
Assistant Editor: Madeleine Samuel
Project Editor: Graham Bateman
Production: Clive Sparling, Joanna
    Turner

Media conversion and typesetting:
    Robert and Peter MacDonald,
    Una Macnamara

AN EQUINOX BOOK

Planned and produced by:
Equinox (Oxford) Limited,
Musterlin House, Jordan Hill Road,
Oxford OX2 8DP, England

Prepared by Lionheart Books

Library of Congress
Cataloging-in-Publication Data
Kerrod, Robin.
Birds: the waterbirds/Robin Kerrod with
contributions by Jill Bailey.
p.   cm. — — (The Encyclopedia of the
    animal world)
Includes index.
Summary: Provides brief descriptions of
birds that live in or near the water.

1. Water birds – Juvenile literature.
[1. Water birds. 2. Birds.]   I. Bailey, Jill.
II. Title. III. Series.

QL676.2.K47 1989   598.29'24 - dc19
88-33318 CIP AC

ISBN 0-8160-1962-2

Published in North America by
Facts On File, Inc.,
460 Park Avenue South,
New York, N.Y. 10016

Origination by Alpha Reprographics Ltd,
Perivale, Middx, England

Printed in Italy.

10 9 8 7 6 5 4 3 2 1

FACT PANEL: Key to symbols denoting general features of animals

SYMBOLS WITH NO WORDS

Activity time

● Nocturnal

◑ Daytime

◒ Dawn/Dusk

○ All the time

Group size

◪ Solitary

▣ Pairs

◼ Small groups (up to 10)

■ Flocks

◢ Variable

Conservation status

☠ All species threatened

☡ Some species threatened

No species threatened (no symbol)

SYMBOLS NEXT TO HEADINGS

Habitat

◥ General

◣ Mountain/Moorland

◢ Desert

▱ Sea

■ Amphibious

◤ Tundra

◤ Forest/Woodland

● Grassland

⊛ Freshwater

Diet

■ Other animals

■ Plants

◪ Animals and Plants

Breeding

◐ Seasonal (at fixed times)

◑ Non-seasonal (at any time)

CONTENTS

PREFACE

The National Wildlife Federation

For the wildlife of the world, 1936 was a very big year. That's when the National Wildlife Federation formed to help conserve the millions of species of animals and plants that call Earth their home. In trying to do such an important job, the Federation has grown to be the largest conservation group of its kind.

Today, plants and animals face more dangers than ever before. As the human population grows and takes over more and more land, the wild places of the world disappear. As people produce more and more chemicals and cars and other products to make life better for themselves, the environment often becomes worse for wildlife.

But there is some good news. Many animals are better off today than when the National Wildlife Federation began. Alligators, wild turkeys, deer, wood ducks, and others are thriving – thanks to the hard work of everyone who cares about wildlife.

The Federation's number one job has always been education. We teach kids the wonders of nature through *Your Big Backyard* and *Ranger Rick* magazines and our annual National Wildlife Week celebration. We teach grown-ups the importance of a clean environment through *National Wildlife* and *International Wildlife* magazines. And we help teachers teach about wildlife with our environmental education activity series called *Naturescope*.

The National Wildlife Federation is nearly five million people, all working as one. We all know that by helping wildlife, we are also helping ourselves. Together we have helped pass laws that have cleaned up our air and water, protected endangered species, and left grand old forests standing tall.

You can help too. Every time you plant a bush that becomes a home to a butterfly, every time you help clean a lake or river of trash, every time you walk instead of asking for a ride in a car – you are part of the wildlife team.

You are also doing your part by learning all you can about the wildlife of the world. That's why the National Wildlife Federation is happy to help bring you this Encyclopedia. We hope you enjoy it.

Jay D. Hair, President
National Wildlife Federation

INTRODUCTION

The Encyclopedia of the Animal World surveys the main groups and species of animals alive today. Written by a team of specialists, it includes the most current information and the newest ideas on animal behavior and survival. The Encyclopedia looks at how the shape and form of an animal reflect its life-style – the ways in which a creature's size, color, feeding methods and defenses have all evolved in relationship to a particular diet, climate and habitat. Discussed also are the ways in which human activities often disrupt natural ecosystems and threaten the survival of many species.

In this Encyclopedia the animals are grouped on the basis of their body structure and their evolution from common ancestors. Thus, there are single volumes or groups of volumes on mammals, birds, reptiles and amphibians, fish, insects and so on. Within these major categories, the animals are grouped according to their feeding habits or general life-styles. Because there is so much information on the animals in two of these major categories, there are four volumes devoted to mammals (The Small Plant-Eaters; The Hunters; The Large Plant-Eaters; Primates, Insect-Eaters and Baleen Whales) and three to birds (The Waterbirds; The Aerial Hunters; The Plant- and Seed-Eaters).

This volume, Birds – The Waterbirds, includes entries on penguins, albatrosses, pelicans, cormorants, herons, flamingos, ducks, plovers, gulls and terns. Together they number some 900 species. Many of them are common around shores and on lakes and reservoirs. Some, such as gulls, breed in huge colonies and build their nests on the narrow ledges of cliff faces. Others, for example swans, are frequently seen in parks. Ducks and geese often live close to people.

Most waterbirds are carnivores, which means that animal material makes up the major part of their food. But their diets vary greatly. Penguins feed on fish, squid and krill, while ducks eat water weeds, seeds, frogs and insects. In general, those species that live and breed on coasts – the seabirds – are strictly carnivores. Those that inhabit inland waters have a diet of animal and plant material – they are omnivores. Important among the latter are birds commonly called waders – the herons, storks and so on – and waterfowl – the ducks, geese and swans.

Many groups of waterbirds are very successful animals, occupying every type of water habitat or having a worldwide distribution. Their success owes much to their ability to travel great distances and to navigate between breeding grounds in the far north, where food is plentiful in spring, and overwintering areas in the south.

This volume also contains an introduction to birds in general, describing and illustrating the unique physical characteristics of this collection of animals.

Each article in this Encyclopedia is devoted to an individual species or group of closely related species. The text starts with a short scene-setting story that highlights one or more of the animal's unique features. It then continues with details of the most interesting aspects of the animal's physical features and abilities, diet and feeding behavior, and general life-style. It also covers conservation and the animal's relationships with people.

A fact panel provides easy reference to the main features of distribution (natural, not introductions to other areas by humans), habitat, diet, size, color and breeding. (An explanation of the color-coded symbols is given on page 2 of the book.) The panel also includes a list of the common and scientific (Latin) names of species mentioned in the main text and photo captions. For species illustrated in major artwork panels but not described elsewhere, the names are given in the caption accompanying the artwork. In such illustrations, all animals are shown to scale; actual dimensions may be found in the text. To help the reader appreciate the size of the animals, in the upper right part of the page at the beginning of an article are scale drawings comparing the size of the species with that of a human being (or of a human foot).

Many species of animal are threatened with extinction as a result of human activities. In this Encyclopedia the following terms are used to show the status of a species as defined by the International Union for the Conservation of Nature and Natural Resources:

Endangered – in danger of extinction unless their habitat is no longer destroyed and they are not hunted by people.

Vulnerable – likely to become endangered in the near future.

Rare – exist in small numbers but neither endangered nor vulnerable at present.

A glossary provides definitions of technical terms used in the book. A common name and scientific (Latin) name index provide easy access to text and illustrations.

WHAT IS A BIRD?

Birds, with their powers of flight, are found in almost every part of the globe. A few birds, such as ostriches and penguins, cannot fly. Instead, the ostrich can run very fast, up to 45mph, and the penguin uses its wings as flippers for swimming.

All birds lay eggs with hard, water-proof shells and a good supply of yolk as food for the developing embryo.

Birds are warm-blooded (ectother-mic), with bodies covered in feathers. They are vertebrates, having an internal bony skeleton with a central backbone or vertebral column for support. The forelimbs are highly modified and take the form of wings. Birds walk on their two hind legs. The legs and feet are covered in scales. The mouth is a horny beak or bill.

▼The bird's smooth, streamlined shape helps it move swiftly through the air. The skeleton is very light – many of the bones are hollow. The breastbone has a large keel to which the powerful flight muscles are attached. The body and wings are covered in feathers, which are light but strong. The lungs lead into a series of air sacs which improve the bird's oxygen supply when flying, as well as making its body lighter. In some birds the air sacs even extend into the legs.

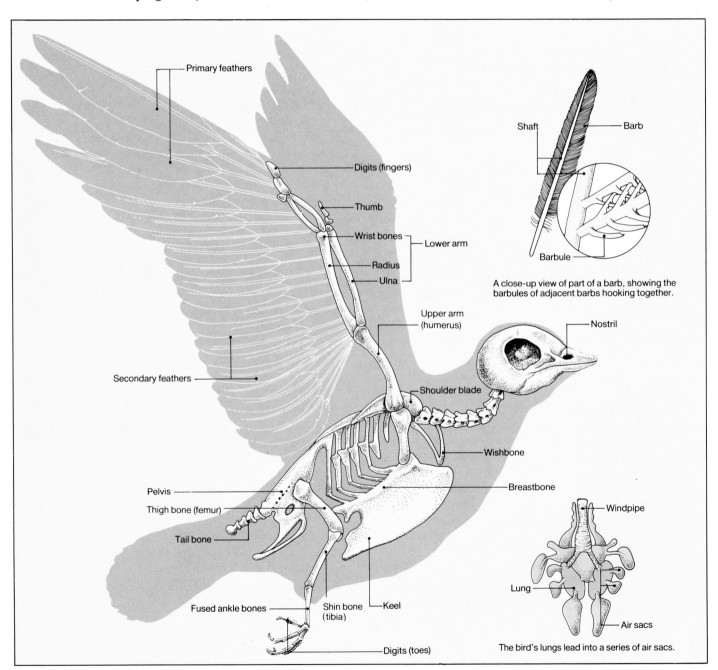

Primary feathers

Digits (fingers)

Thumb

Wrist bones — Lower arm

Radius

Ulna

Upper arm (humerus)

Shoulder blade

Secondary feathers

Wishbone

Pelvis

Breastbone

Thigh bone (femur)

Tail bone

Fused ankle bones

Shin bone (tibia)

Keel

Digits (toes)

Shaft — Barb

Barbule

A close-up view of part of a barb, showing the barbules of adjacent barbs hooking together.

Nostril

Windpipe

Lung

Air sacs

The bird's lungs lead into a series of air sacs.

FEATHERS

Birds are the only animals that have feathers. The feathers are of different shapes and sizes according to their position on the body and therefore their function. The wing feathers, for example, are long, stiff, and slightly curved to improve the bird's stream-lining. A chick's down feathers have no definite shape. A very small bird, such as a hummingbird, may have about 900 feathers, while a large bird like a swan may have over 25,000.

Feathers are made of keratin, the same material that forms hair, nails and, in reptiles, scales. Each feather has a stiff hollow shaft with hundreds of side branches called barbs. Each barb has two rows of barbules. The hooks of one row lock into furrows on the next row. This keeps the feather stiff and flat. Feathers are lightweight because of all the air spaces between the barbules.

Feathers also help to keep the bird warm. Air trapped between them prevents the bird's body heat escaping. Baby birds have soft fluffy down feathers for extra warmth. Some adult birds that live in cold regions also have an underlayer of down.

When preening, the bird runs its beak along its feathers to "zip up" the barbules. It rubs oil on the feathers from a special gland under the tail to make them waterproof. Once or twice a year, birds shed their old, worn feathers and grow new ones. This is called molting.

▶The feet of some birds are adapted for swimming, with flaps of skin called webs to give a bigger area for pushing against the water. In ducks, the web stretches right across the foot, while in moorhens it is just a flap along the base of the toes. Grebes have lobed toes instead. Penguins use their wings as flippers, as if they are flying underwater.

▼Beaks come in many shapes and sizes. Birds have no teeth. Hawks, however, can tear up pieces of meat. Parrots use their beak like an extra foot when climbing. Flamingos have tooth-like edges to their bill for sieving food from the water. Finches can crack open hard seeds, while pelicans can store several fish in their throat pouch.

BEAKS GALORE

A bird's beak is often a special shape and size to deal with a particular kind of food. Some birds feed on meat or fish, others on leaves, flowers, seeds or fruit. Hummingbirds sip liquid nectar from flowers. A few birds, like flamingos, sieve food from the water of lakes and rivers. Several birds, such as seagulls, will eat almost anything.

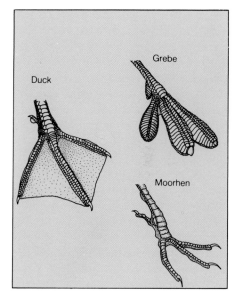

Duck

Grebe

Moorhen

▼The young chick grows inside a little bag of fluid, the amnion. The yolk and albumen are a source of food for the chick. Its blood vessels spread out over the yolk sac to absorb the food. The chick's waste is stored in another little bag, the allantois, until hatching.

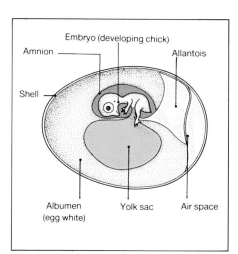

Embryo (developing chick)

Amnion

Allantois

Shell

Albumen (egg white)

Yolk sac

Air space

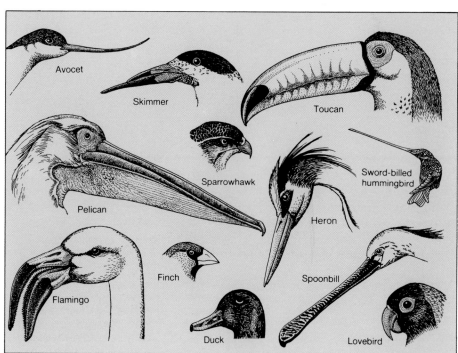

Avocet

Skimmer

Toucan

Pelican

Sparrowhawk

Sword-billed hummingbird

Heron

Finch

Flamingo

Spoonbill

Duck

Lovebird

BIRD SENSE

Birds have excellent eyesight, often better than human sight. They have an extra transparent eyelid to protect their eyes from dust and rain while flying. Most birds have a poor sense of smell, but excellent hearing. A bird's ears are hidden under feathers at the side of its head.

COURTSHIP AND BREEDING

Birds usually become interested in courting only at a time of year when there is going to be plenty of food around to feed to the young. First, the male bird looks for a mate. He shows off to any females he meets, dancing, calling and fluffing out his feathers. Male birds are often more brightly colored than the females, and their displays show off their plumage. The female is usually dull colored so that she will be camouflaged while she is sitting on her nest.

Many male birds defend a special feeding area – a territory – during the breeding season. This makes sure they can feed their family. For small birds, the territory may be just the area immediately around the nest, but large birds of prey may defend an area of 8sq miles.

FROM EGG TO ADULT

Birds usually build nests in which to lay their eggs. The nest may be just a scrape in the ground lined with grass and leaves, or a cup of twigs or moss high in a tree or on a cliff ledge, out of reach of predators.

The baby birds grow inside the eggs for several weeks before hatching. During this time, the eggs must be kept warm, so the parent birds must sit on the nest to "incubate" them.

Birds such as chickens, which nest on the ground, usually have well-developed young. They hatch already covered in fluffy down, and can run around and feed themselves almost at once. But the young of many birds hatch naked and blind, and have to be fed by their parents for several weeks. Gradually, they grow a warm fluffy coat of down, and later a coat of proper feathers.

LIVING FLYING MACHINES

The bird's wings are really forelimbs: they have the same bones as the human arm, but some bones in the wrist and fingers are fused together for extra strength. Some of the bones of the back are also fused together to withstand the beating of the wings.

There is more than one way of flying. Small birds, with plump bodies and rather short wings, have to flap a lot to stay airborne, but larger birds with long, narrow wings can make greater use of air currents and gliding.

LONG-DISTANCE TRAVELERS

Some birds spend the summer in one part of the world and the winter in another to take advantage of seasonal food supplies. Swallows, for example, rear their families in northern Europe and North America in summer, when insects are plentiful, but fly south in the fall as the insects disappear. Such journeys are called migration.

▶ *Archaeopteryx* was part bird, part reptile. Its body was covered in feathers, but it had a long tail, jaws with teeth, a small breastbone, and claws on its wings. It probably lived in trees, using its claws for scrambling among branches.

▲ As the Blue tit beats down with its wings, the force of the air spreads and bends its feathers.

ANCESTORS OF BIRDS

Birds are believed to be descended from small dinosaurs. Today, the most obvious clue to their reptile ancestry is the scales on their legs and feet. Some of their ancestors had large overlapping scales to help keep them warm. These scales may well have evolved into feathers. There are very few bird fossils. The oldest is *Archaeopteryx*, 150 million years old.

BIRD FACTS

About 8,805 species

Weight Smallest, Bee hummingbird, 1/18 ounce; largest, ostrich, 340lb.

Eggs Largest, ostrich, 8in long, 4lb; smallest, Vervain hummingbird, 1/2in, 1/80 ounce.

Most feathers Whistling swan, 25,000+.

Fastest flying bird White-throated spine-tail swift, 110mph.

Longest lifespan Sulphur-crested cockatoo, 80+ years.

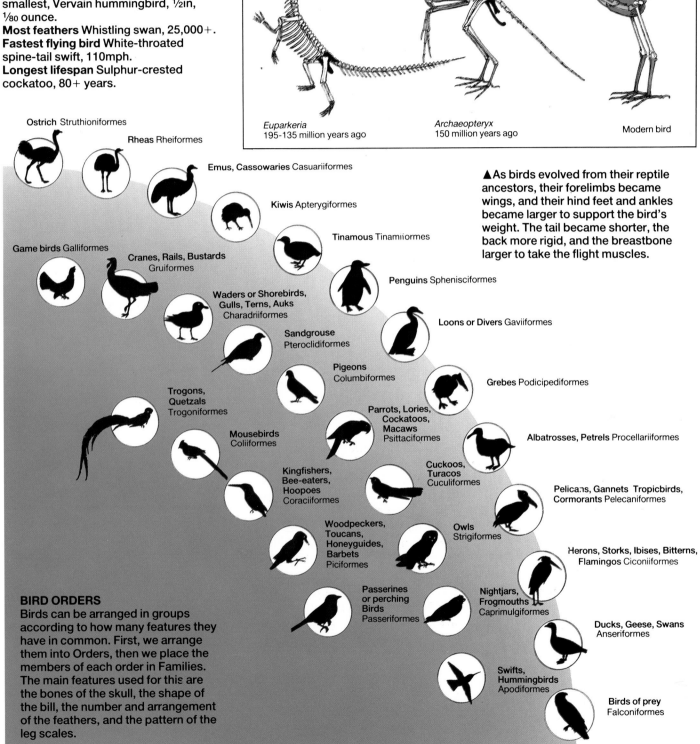

Euparkeria
195-135 million years ago

Archaeopteryx
150 million years ago

Modern bird

▲As birds evolved from their reptile ancestors, their forelimbs became wings, and their hind feet and ankles became larger to support the bird's weight. The tail became shorter, the back more rigid, and the breastbone larger to take the flight muscles.

Ostrich Struthioniformes

Rheas Rheiformes

Emus, Cassowaries Casuariiformes

Kiwis Apterygiformes

Tinamous Tinamiiformes

Game birds Galliformes

Cranes, Rails, Bustards Gruiformes

Waders or Shorebirds, Gulls, Terns, Auks Charadriiformes

Penguins Sphenisciformes

Loons or Divers Gaviiformes

Sandgrouse Pteroclidiformes

Pigeons Columbiformes

Grebes Podicipediformes

Trogons, Quetzals Trogoniformes

Parrots, Lories, Cockatoos, Macaws Psittaciformes

Albatrosses, Petrels Procellariiformes

Mousebirds Coliiformes

Kingfishers, Bee-eaters, Hoopoes Coraciiformes

Cuckoos, Turacos Cuculiformes

Pelicans, Gannets Tropicbirds, Cormorants Pelecaniformes

Woodpeckers, Toucans, Honeyguides, Barbets Piciformes

Owls Strigiformes

Herons, Storks, Ibises, Bitterns, Flamingos Ciconiiformes

BIRD ORDERS

Birds can be arranged in groups according to how many features they have in common. First, we arrange them into Orders, then we place the members of each order in Families. The main features used for this are the bones of the skull, the shape of the bill, the number and arrangement of the feathers, and the pattern of the leg scales.

Passerines or perching Birds Passeriformes

Nightjars, Frogmouths Caprimulgiformes

Ducks, Geese, Swans Anseriformes

Swifts, Hummingbirds Apodiformes

Birds of prey Falconiformes

9

PENGUINS

Just off shore what look like porpoises are rippling through the icy water, first leaping into the air and then diving. As they come closer one can see that they are not porpoises at all. They are penguins swimming fast, performing what is called "porpoising."

Penguins are the most common of all the flightless birds, but unlike most of the others they are skilled swimmers. They are found most widely along the coast of Antarctica and in the surrounding waters of the Southern Ocean. Some species, however, live farther north, even as far as equatorial regions.

Four of the best-known species are the Emperor, Adelie, Chinstrap and Rockhopper penguins. The first three always stay in the Antarctic, while the

Rockhopper ranges farther north to more temperate regions.

The Emperor, the largest of the penguins, is almost twice as big as the other three species. It has distinctive orange-yellow patches on the sides of its head and throat. Its close, but slightly smaller relative, the King penguin, has similar markings.

The Chinstrap penguin is so-called because of a black band around its throat. The Adelie has a sharp head and white eye-rings. To most people

▼ ▶ **Species of penguin and their activities** Two nearly full-grown chicks stand with an adult Yellow-eyed penguin (*Megadyptes antipodes*) (**1**). Rockhopper penguin (**2**) parents with young. Note their distinctive head crests. Two male King penguins (**3**) incubating eggs under a flap of skin near their feet. One is using its bill to arrange the position of the egg.

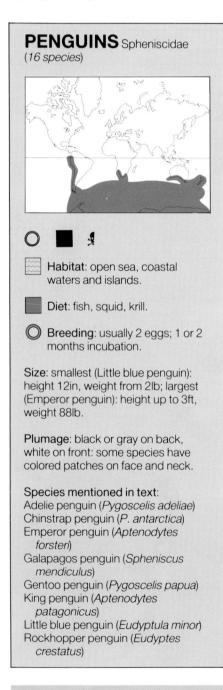

PENGUINS Spheniscidae
(*16 species*)

○ ■ 🐾

〰 Habitat: open sea, coastal waters and islands.

▪ Diet: fish, squid, krill.

◎ Breeding: usually 2 eggs; 1 or 2 months incubation.

Size: smallest (Little blue penguin): height 12in, weight from 2lb; largest (Emperor penguin): height up to 3ft, weight 88lb.

Plumage: black or gray on back, white on front: some species have colored patches on face and neck.

Species mentioned in text:
Adelie penguin (*Pygoscelis adeliae*)
Chinstrap penguin (*P. antarctica*)
Emperor penguin (*Aptenodytes forsteri*)
Galapagos penguin (*Spheniscus mendiculus*)
Gentoo penguin (*Pygoscelis papua*)
King penguin (*Aptenodytes patagonicus*)
Little blue penguin (*Eudyptula minor*)
Rockhopper penguin (*Eudyptes crestatus*)

▲A Gentoo penguin carries grass back to its nest. Like most penguins it nests in huge colonies, often some way inland.

the typical penguin, it is found widely in zoos. The Rockhopper is named for its comical-looking hopping walk. It is one of the crested penguins, with long yellow tufts on the sides of the head.

SUPREME SWIMMERS

On land, penguins move very awkwardly and, to humans, comically. Their feet are set well back on the body, and they walk with a clumsy waddle or a hop. Going downhill on ice and snow, they often slide on their bellies to move faster. This is called "toboganning." Penguins cannot fold away their short stubby wings like ordinary birds, so these constantly flap about.

However, when penguins enter their natural element, the sea, they become graceful and swift movers. They have a beautifully streamlined body and use their wings, or flippers, as paddles to propel themselves through the water. They use their webbed feet as a rudder to change

►Two Adelie penguins greet each other (4). Adelies often "toboggan" in the snow (5). When swimming, the Adelie may skim the surface like a porpoise (6). Then it leaps out of the water (7). The Jackass penguin (Spheniscus demersus), pictured standing (8) and swimming ashore (9), is named after its braying call.

direction and also as a brake to slow them down.

The penguin's body is covered with a dense coat of three layers of short oily feathers. This keeps the body dry underneath and acts as insulation to keep in the body heat. A layer of fat, or blubber, beneath the skin also helps protect the bird from the ice-cold water.

FEEDING TIME
All species of penguin feed in the water. Some, including the Gentoo penguin, feed mainly on fish near the surface. Others, including the King and Emperor penguins, often dive deep for prey such as squid. Emperors have been known to remain underwater for over 15 minutes and to dive deeper than 850ft. It is not known how these birds can dive to such a depth, where the water pressure is high, without suffering from "the bends." This is a painful and often dangerous condition human divers experience if they surface too quickly after a deep dive.

Most penguins do not feed at all times of the year. When they are breeding they may go for weeks or, in the case of the Emperor penguin, months without feeding. So before the breeding season begins, penguins feed constantly to build up a reserve of fat. During the fasting period they may lose nearly half their body weight.

BREEDING TIME
Penguins that live in warmer climates sometimes breed twice a year. These species include the Galapagos penguin of the Galapagos Islands on the equator. But the majority of penguin species breed in the spring, which in the Southern Hemisphere means during the months of September and October.

The Adelie penguin, for example, returns to its nesting grounds in October. Like most other species, males and females usually pair up with their partner of the previous year. They build a nest of pebbles and the female lays two eggs. After about 40 days of incubation, the chicks are hatched. Both parents feed them by regurgitation – swallowing food and bringing it up again. By February or March the chicks have molted their thick downy coat and acquired adult plumage. Then they head for the sea and become independent.

Curiously, the Emperor penguin breeds in Arctic midwinter, when the temperature drops to −100°F and below, and winds blow at speeds of up to 50mph. Breeding colonies form in the fall (mid-May). The female lays a single egg on the ice. The male incubates the egg, tucking it under a flap of skin on its belly. Emperors keep warm themselves by huddling together. In some colonies as many as 6,000 birds may do this. When the chick hatches, one of the parents carries it on its feet to keep the chick off the frozen ground.

◀The only time penguins "fly" is when they dive into the sea. Here Adelie penguins launch themselves from the edge of the ice.

▶A colony of King penguins. Each incubates an egg under its bulging lower belly for about 2 months.

12

LOONS OR DIVERS

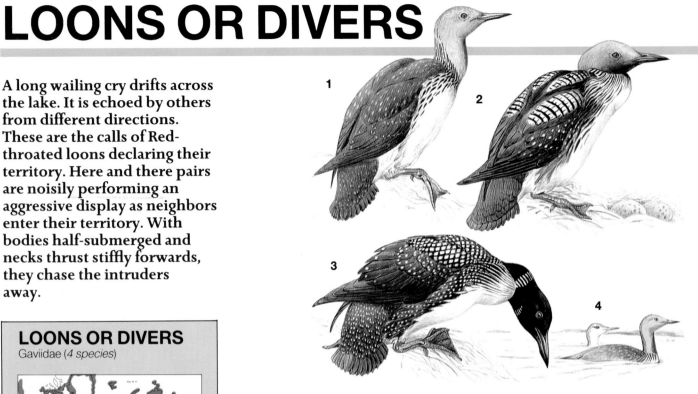

A long wailing cry drifts across the lake. It is echoed by others from different directions. These are the calls of Red-throated loons declaring their territory. Here and there pairs are noisily performing an aggressive display as neighbors enter their territory. With bodies half-submerged and necks thrust stiffly forwards, they chase the intruders away.

LOONS OR DIVERS
Gaviidae (4 species)

 Habitat: freshwater lakes in summer, usually sea coasts in winter.

Diet: fish, crustaceans, frogs.

Breeding: usually 2 eggs; 24-29 days incubation.

Size: smallest (Red-throated diver): length from 20in, weight 2lb; largest (White-billed diver): length up to 3ft, weight 14lb.

Plumage: black or brown back and white belly; often white stripes on neck and white spots on back. Red-throated loon has red throat in summer.

Species mentioned in text:
Black-throated loon (*Gavia arctica*)
Common loon (*G. immer*)
Red-throated loon (*G. stellata*)
Yellow-billed loon (*G. adamsii*)

The Red-throated loon always has its head tilted slightly upwards. This is one way it can be distinguished in winter from its slightly bigger relative, the Black-throated or Arctic loon. In winter both have similar plumage, brown on the back and white on the belly. So also do the other two species of loon, the Common and the Yellow-billed loons.

The loons, called divers throughout Europe, breed in the far north. The Common loon, or Great northern diver, breeds only in arctic North America; the Yellow-billed loon almost only in arctic Europe and Asia. But the other two species breed in all these locations. All species migrate south for the winter, a few even as far as southern Europe and the southern United States.

GOING FISHING
Loons are superb swimmers; they have streamlined bodies and strong webbed feet set well back. They spend little time on land, where they can move only clumsily. They feed underwater, chasing and catching fish with an easy grace. As well as fish, they take frogs, crustaceans and worms. They dive regularly to depths of 30ft and

▲Summer plumage Red-throated loon (1): rust-red throat, gray head and brown back. Black-throated loon (2): gray head, black back and white stripes on neck and wings. Common loon (3): glossy green-black head and neck, neck patch of black and white bands, and white-spotted black back. At times loons swim with their bodies almost submerged (4).

occasionally much deeper. They can adjust their buoyancy – the way they float in the water – by adjusting the amount of air in their feathers, air sacs and lungs. They can stay submerged for up to several minutes.

The food loons catch is being greatly affected by pollution, in the form of pesticides and acid rain. And this is causing them to alter their feeding sites and range. In many parts of Europe and North America, their numbers are also declining as their habitats are disturbed or destroyed by human development. Large numbers are also at risk because of oil pollution at their coastal wintering sites.

NESTING
Divers are usually solitary nesters, although the Red-throated and Arctic loons sometimes nest in colonies. They nest on bare lake shores or

low-lying islands, where they are safe from most predators. They lay their eggs on the ground or in a crude nest of water-weed. The eggs are olive green to dark brown in color and are incubated by both parents.

The chicks emerge well-developed and leave the nest within a day of hatching. They often ride on their parents' backs. Their parents catch food for them and feed it to them fresh, not regurgitated. The chicks begin catching prey for themselves before they are 2 weeks old.

▼The beautiful head of the Black-throated or Arctic loon, showing its neck stripes. It is streamlined for swimming efficiently underwater.

►The Common loon swims with powerful thrusts of its webbed feet. At the end of one stroke (top) it streaks through the water like a dart. As it brings its feet forward for another thrust, its head stays more or less still in the water. This allows it to detect prey more easily. It then extends its neck as it gives another thrust (bottom).

GREBES

As two Great-crested grebes approach each other on the water, one dives underneath and then surfaces close to its mate. It rises up out of the water in a "ghostly penguin" display. Its mate draws in its head and fluffs out its feathers like a cat raises its hair when it's frightened.

The penguin and cat displays of a pair of Great-crested grebes form the first part of a complicated courtship between them. It is the "discovery" ceremony. Both birds have their dark crests and head ruffs extended.

Afterwards the pair, swimming side by side, preen themselves before launching into the most spectacular display of all, the weed ceremony. They swim away from each other and gather weeds in their bills. Then they turn and swim swiftly towards each other. Just before they meet they rise up out of the water and present weeds to each other face to face.

Many of the other grebes perform similar ceremonies, but not as strikingly. Another good performer, the Slavonian grebe, has a summer plumage of chestnut neck and flanks and golden ear tufts, which give it the alternative name of Horned grebe.

DIVING TO FEED

Grebes are excellent swimmers and divers. They have dense, watertight

---

GREBES Podicipedidae
(*20 species*)

[map]

● ▣ 🦈

🌊 **Habitat:** freshwater ponds, lakes and marshes.

▪ **Diet:** water insects, crustaceans, molluscs and fish.

◎ **Breeding:** up to 6 white or cream-colored eggs; 20-30 days incubation.

Size: smallest (Little grebe): length from 13½in, weight 4½ ounces; largest (Great-crested grebe): length up to 1½ft, weight 3lb.

Plumage: brown or gray back, with white underbelly; some have reddish-orange markings on neck and face; some have crests or ear tufts.

Species mentioned in text:
Atitlan grebe (*Podilymbus gigas*)
Great-crested grebe (*Podiceps cristatus*)
Little grebe (*Tachybaptus ruficollis*)
Pied-billed grebe (*Podilymbus podiceps*)
Slavonian grebe (*Podiceps auritus*)
Western grebe (*Aechmorphorus occidentalis*)

---

plumage with hardly any tail. They have broad lobes on their toes, which act as paddles to propel them when swimming. They can expel air from their feathers and air sacs to sink low in the water when they come across something suspicious. They do the same when they dive.

Most grebes dive to feed in the top few feet of the water. The Great-crested grebe usually feeds in open water, chasing fish. The Little grebe feeds mainly on insects and crustaceans in and around water-plants in ponds and shallow bays. This attractive bird, which constantly dives and bobs, is also known as the dabchick.

RELUCTANT FLYERS

Grebes, like penguins, walk clumsily on land. They can get stranded if they land on a wet road, mistaking it for a river. Most grebes also do not fly well and avoid doing so. To fly, they need a long pattering take-off over the water.

Some grebes, however, undertake long flights when migrating. These include the Western, Slavonian and Pied-billed grebes, which summer in

▼Part of the courtship display carried out by a mating pair of Great-crested grebes. First comes the discovery ceremony (1), followed by head-shaking (2) and preening (3). The display's climax is the weed ceremony (4).

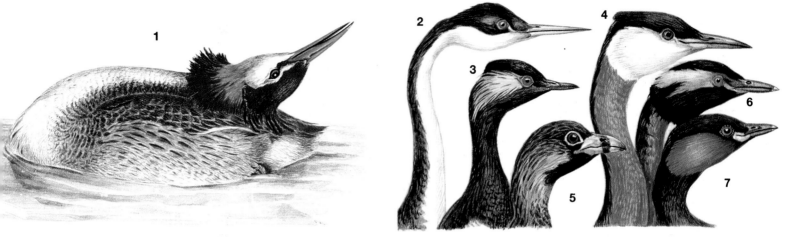

▲Grebe family neck and head patterns
The Great-crested grebe **(1)** has a neck ruff and head crest. The neck of the Western grebe is long and arched, hence its other name of Swan grebe **(2)**. Black-necked grebe (*Podiceps nigricollis*) **(3)** and the Red-necked grebe (*P. grisegena*) **(4)**. Also the Pied-billed grebe **(5)**, Slavonian grebe **(6)** and Little grebe **(7)**.

the far north and fly south to avoid the winter cold. They often travel by night. The Western grebe is also notable for its method of fishing – spearing fish with its sharp bill rather than grabbing them with it.

A few grebes are flightless. They include several rare species, like the Atitlan grebe, which lives only on certain lakes in Central and South America.

ON THE NEST
Both sexes share in raising the young, building nests of reeds and water-weed on the water. Nests may be anchored to the reeds at the bottom or free floating. Some species, including the Little grebe, may raise as many as three broods a year if food supplies are unusually good.

Eggs are laid at intervals, and the birds start incubating them before the clutch is complete. When the birds have to leave the nest while incubating, they cover the eggs with weeds to hide them and keep them warm. The chicks hatch at intervals and at first are carried on their parents' backs in the nest, when swimming and even when they dive.

▶A male Great-crested grebe visits its mate, incubating the eggs.

ALBATROSSES

Out in the middle of the ocean a lone albatross is following a ship, waiting for food scraps to be thrown overboard. It has been circling around for hours, back and forth, at speeds of up to 60mph. Amazingly, no one on board the ship has ever seen the bird flap its wings.

ALBATROSSES
Diomedeidae (*14 species*)

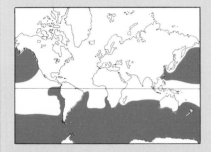

  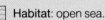

~~~ Habitat: open sea.

■ Diet: fish, crustaceans.

◎ Breeding: 1 white egg; 65-79 days incubation.

Size: smallest (mollymawks): length from 27in, wingspan 6ft; largest (great albatrosses): length up to 4½ft, wingspan 11½ft.

Plumage: varies, from white with dark wing tips (great albatrosses) to all-over dark, sooty brown (Sooty albatross).

Species mentioned in text:
Black-browed albatross (*Diomedea melanophris*)
Black-footed albatross (*D. nigripes*)
Laysan albatross (*D. immutabilis*)
Light-mantled sooty albatross (*Phoebetria palpebrata*)
Royal albatross (*Diomedea epomophora*)
Sooty albatross (*Phoebetria fusca*)
Wandering albatross (*Diomedea exulans*)
Waved albatross (*D. irrorata*)

With their long narrow wings, albatrosses are among the most skilled gliders in the bird world. They ride the air currents with scarcely any effort. Found mainly in the great Southern Ocean to the south of South America, Africa and Australia, they revel in the strong winds that blow there.

Outstanding species are the Wandering and Royal albatrosses, often called the great albatrosses. They have enormous wings which, in the Wandering albatross, have an average span of over 10ft. The Wandering albatross nests mainly on islands near the Antarctic Circle and in the South Atlantic. The Royal albatross nests on islands near New Zealand and southern South America.

THE MOLLYMAWKS
Most albatrosses are tame, allowing people to approach and even stroke them. Because of this, the birds were called mollymawks ("stupid gulls") by early sailors. This name is now often used for some of the smaller species such as the Black-footed albatross, which has a wingspan of only about 4ft. Sooty-brown all over, it nests on tropical islands in the North Pacific. Another tropical island breeder is the Waved albatross, which nests only in the Galapagos Islands.

Between the great albatrosses and mollymawks in size are the two species of dark-brown sooty albatrosses which have a 6½ft-wingspan.

All albatrosses have a strong bill hooked at the end. Like shearwaters and petrels, they have tubed nostrils, one on each side of the bill. Also, they

▼A pair of young Laysan albatrosses trying to incubate a grapefruit. They do not seem to know what an egg looks like.

produce large amounts of oil in their gut. They bring up this oil when regurgitating food for their young.

LONG-LIVED SLOW DEVELOPER

Albatrosses are among the longest-living birds. Some have been known to live for over 50 years, although 30 years is a more typical lifespan. They are capable of breeding at 3 or 4 years old, but they do not usually start for several years after this. Some individuals may not breed until they are 15 years old.

Most albatrosses nest in large colonies, on the bare ground or on mounds of dirt and vegetation. Mating occurs after long courtship displays, which may involve bowing, wing-stretching, bill-fencing and dancing. After hatching, the albatross chick spends from 4 to 9 months on the nest site before its flight feathers form and it can start to fly. The Wandering albatross has a total nesting period (incubation plus fledging) of nearly a year.

Albatrosses were once under threat. People killed them in huge numbers for their feathers and meat. Sailors once believed that it was bad luck to kill albatrosses, which were supposed to carry the souls of the drowned. Today, most colonies are thriving, since they are located mainly on remote islands where they have few natural enemies.

▲A Wandering albatross reacts angrily to the presence of two seals, or maybe the photographer. Most of the species build high nests like this.

►The name of the Light-mantled sooty albatross describes its color well (1). The parents take turns feeding and guarding the single chick. The Black-browed albatross does not take to the air until it is nearly 4 months old. The picture shows a young bird in flight (2).

SHEARWATERS

A fox moves stealthily up to the fulmar resting on the rocky shore. Just as it is about to pounce, the fulmar sees it. The bird lets loose a jet of stinking oil into the predator's face. Surprised, the fox starts back, giving time for the fulmar to make good its escape.

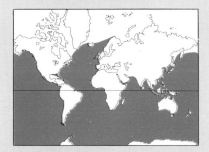

SHEARWATERS
Procellariidae, Hydrobatidae, Pelecanoididae (*78 species*)

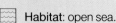 Habitat: open sea.

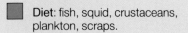 Diet: fish, squid, crustaceans, plankton, scraps.

Breeding: 1 white egg, sometimes speckled; 40-60 days incubation.

Size: smallest (storm petrels): length from 5½in, wingspan 1ft; largest (giant petrels): length up to 35in, wingspan 6½ft.

Plumage: most species black or gray back, pale underwings.

Species mentioned in text:
Bermuda petrel (*Pterodroma cahow*)
Georgian diving petrel (*Pelecanoides georgicus*)
Hall's giant petrel (*Macronectes halli*)
Manx shearwater (*Puffinus puffinus*)
Northern fulmar (*Fulmarus glacialis*)
Short-tailed shearwater (*Puffinus tenuirostris*)
Southern fulmar (*Fulmarus glacialis*)
Southern giant petrel (*Macronectes giganteus*)

Most of the other shearwaters, and the related petrels, share the ability of the fulmar to squirt oil at intruders. The main use of their stomach oil, however, is to nourish their young.

The shearwaters are a large family of birds that range from the Arctic to the Antarctic. They include four groups: fulmars, prions, gadfly petrels and true shearwaters. The fulmars are the largest species. They include the Northern and Southern fulmars and the Southern giant petrel, also called the stinker because of its habit of squirting unwelcome visitors.

The prions are the smallest species, also known as whale birds from their habit of following whales. They breed in far southern waters. The gadfly petrels are larger (up to about 1½ft) and are so-called because their flight is more rapid than that of other petrels. They nest in tropical and subtropical regions and include the rare Burmuda petrel, which occurs only on that island.

LONG-DISTANCE TRAVEL
Shearwaters are named after their habit of skimming the surface of the sea, seeming to "shear" the waves. The true shearwaters, of the *Puffinus* genus, are superb navigators. Some species travel vast distances during their annual migration.

The common Manx shearwater breeds not only on the Isle of Man, but also in the Mediterranean, North America and New Zealand. Some British Manx shearwaters spend the winter off South America. The Short-tailed shearwater travels even farther. From its breeding grounds in southern Australia, it travels all the way round the Pacific Ocean, a distance of some 18,000 miles.

▼A Hall's giant petrel on the nest. It has the typical tube nose of the petrels on top of its powerful bill. The bird feeds only at sea, and its diet consists mainly of large fish and squid. Its bill is also equipped with sharp hooks for holding prey securely.

NESTING IN MILLIONS

Most shearwaters and petrels nest in huge colonies. On the island of South Georgia there are estimated to be up to two million breeding pairs of Georgian diving petrels.

The fulmars usually nest in the open in a simple scrape in the ground or on a cliff ledge. Many of the other species nest in burrows in the ground, under rocks and even under tree roots. These species often come and go at night to avoid predators. Breeding pairs usually stay together year after year, returning usually independently to the same nest site.

The single egg the birds lay is extremely large relative to their body size. Storm petrels may lay eggs weighing up to a quarter of their body weight. Because the egg is so large, it takes great energy to produce; the birds cannot lay again if an egg is lost.

The young birds leave their nests after about 2 weeks. They do not breed until about 4 years old.

▶ **Species of petrel** The Southern giant petrel (1) is feeding on a dead seal. Its wingspan of up to 6½ft is nearly four times that of Wilson's storm petrel (*Oceanites oceanicus*) (2), known as a storm petrel from its habit of sheltering beside ships during a storm. The Gray-backed storm petrel (*Garrodia nereis*) (3) has paler plumage. The Common diving petrel (*Pelecanoides urinatrix*) (4) has a similar body size to the storm petrels. It uses its small wings as paddles when diving to feed.

PELICANS

The Great white pelicans are swimming on the lake looking for a meal. Finding a shoal of fish, they arrange themselves into a horseshoe formation and swim quickly forwards. This drives the fish in a panic towards the center. Then, as if by a secret signal, the pelicans all plunge their bills into the water to catch their herded prey. The birds swallow their food before flying off.

▼ Great white pelicans may live and nest in huge colonies of tens of thousands. The doubled-back neck position in flight is typical of pelicans.

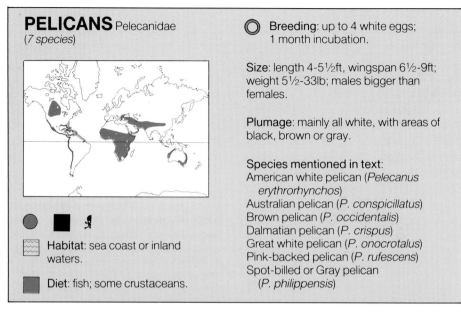

PELICANS Pelecanidae
(*7 species*)

◎ **Breeding**: up to 4 white eggs; 1 month incubation.

Size: length 4-5½ft, wingspan 6½-9ft; weight 5½-33lb; males bigger than females.

Plumage: mainly all white, with areas of black, brown or gray.

Species mentioned in text:
American white pelican (*Pelecanus erythrorhynchos*)
Australian pelican (*P. conspicillatus*)
Brown pelican (*P. occidentalis*)
Dalmatian pelican (*P. crispus*)
Great white pelican (*P. onocrotalus*)
Pink-backed pelican (*P. rufescens*)
Spot-billed or Gray pelican (*P. philippensis*)

● ■ ⬦

▨ Habitat: sea coast or inland waters.

▨ Diet: fish; some crustaceans.

Pelicans are among the largest flying birds, with a bulky body and sturdy webbed feet. But their most outstanding feature is their bill. It is flat, very long and straight, with a hook at the end. Beneath the lower jaw is a fold of elastic skin which can expand into a deep pouch. The pelican does not use this enormous pouch ("which can hold more than its belly can") to store food, as some people think. It uses the pouch for fishing.

As the pelican thrusts its bill into the water to catch a fish, the pouch opens up to form a large scoop. The bird sweeps up the fish in its pouch, together with 18 pints or more of water. It then closes the bill and raises its head from the water. At the same time the skin of the pouch contracts, forcing the water from the pouch, but not the fish. The pelican then lifts up its bill and swallows the fish whole.

In several species, groups of pelicans often fish together, forming a so-called "scare line" to herd schools of fish. The exception is the Brown pelican, which feeds by itself by diving at its prey from the air.

TAKING FLIGHT
Pelicans live only in temperate and tropical regions of the world. Their bodies are not well insulated from the cold, which forces the northern species to migrate south in winter.

Although they are large and ungainly birds which move awkwardly on land, they are skilled flyers. They have many air sacs in their bodies, which makes them exceptionally light for their size. And they can soar effortlessly on the air currents and cover long distances with ease. Some species often travel hundreds of miles daily between remote nesting sites and their lake feeding grounds.

▼The Brown pelican of the Americas has more distinctive coloring than the others, which becomes more intense in the breeding season. It feeds mainly on sea coasts, rather than inland.

▲The Brown pelican dives for its food from the air. After sighting its prey **(1)**, it draws in its wings and dives fast **(2, 3)**. As its bill enters the water, its wings and legs are thrust back **(4)**. It captures its prey in its open bill and greatly expanded pouch **(5)**.

NESTING SITES

All pelicans nest in colonies, often in huge numbers. The four mainly white species (American white, Australian, Dalmatian and Great white) all nest on the ground. They build simple nests of mud, twigs and weeds. The remaining species (Spot-billed, Brown and Pink-backed) which are mainly brown in color, nest in low trees. They build platforms of twigs and branches.

In temperate regions pelicans breed seasonally, in the spring. But in the tropics they may breed at any time of the year. On average they lay only one or two eggs. Both sexes help in incubating and in feeding the chicks when they hatch. The parents feed the chicks by regurgitating partly digested fish into the pouch. The chicks put their heads inside the pouch to eat.

If the parents cannot supply sufficient food for all the nestlings, it is usually the last birds to hatch – and therefore the smallest of the brood – that starve. Nevertheless, the majority of the young do not survive their first year out of the nest.

DISTURBING NEWS

In general pelicans are very sensitive to disturbance. Whole colonies numbering thousands can forsake a nesting site if it is disturbed. Human disturbance and the destruction of habitats have in some regions led to a drastic decline in the numbers and range of some species. Severely at risk at the present time are the Dalmatian pelican of eastern Europe and China, and the Spot-billed pelican of India and Sri Lanka. Both species have been reduced to fewer than 1,500 breeding pairs. A decline in food availability due to over-fishing by humans, and pesticide poisoning, are additional threats to these, and all, pelicans.

▶A group of Australian pelicans expecting a feed. Like white pelicans the world over, they nest in colonies on the ground.

GANNETS AND BOOBIES

A gannet, hungry after its stint incubating on the nest, flies out to sea. It spots a shoal of fish and climbs high above it with powerful beats of its long, pointed wings. Then, with eyes fixed on the fish far below, it dives vertically downwards, dropping like a stone. At high speed it plunges into the waves, emerging seconds later with a well-earned meal.

GANNETS AND BOOBIES Sulidae (9 species)

⬤ ◼ 🐦

🌊 **Habitat:** open sea, islands for breeding.

◼ **Diet:** fish, squid, scraps.

◎ **Breeding:** up to 4 whitish eggs; 42-55 days incubation.

Size: length 2-3ft; wingspan 4½-5½ft; weight 2-8lb; females bigger than males.

Plumage: some mainly white, with gray, brown or black wings or wing tips; other species have dark wings and back.

Species mentioned in text:
Abbott's booby (*Sula abbotti*)
Atlantic gannet (*Morus bassana*)
Australasian gannet (*M. serrator*)
Blue-footed booby (*Sula nebouxii*)
Brown booby (*S. leucogaster*)
Cape or African gannet (*Morus capensis*)
Peruvian booby (*Sula variegata*)
Red-footed booby (*S. sula*)
White booby (*S. dactylatra*)

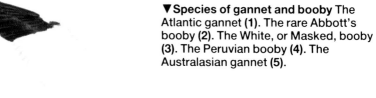

▼**Species of gannet and booby** The Atlantic gannet (**1**). The rare Abbott's booby (**2**). The White, or Masked, booby (**3**). The Peruvian booby (**4**). The Australasian gannet (**5**).

All the gannets and the closely related boobies are known for their spectacular plunge-diving. They are often known as sulids after their family name Sulidae.

The sulids have similarly shaped bodies which are well adapted for their method of fishing. The head is smooth, the body tapered, and the tail long and pointed. The bill is long and has jagged edges for gripping prey. The nostrils are recessed and are closed when diving underwater.

The largest of the sulids is the Atlantic gannet, which is mainly white with black on the wing tips. It has a buff-colored head and nape. The young, however, are darker, taking up to 3 years to acquire the adult plumage. The Australasian and Cape or African gannets are very similar.

TROPICAL CLOWNS

The boobies live in the tropics. They get their name from their "stupidity" in allowing humans to get close to them. This trusting behavior has led over the centuries to millions of the birds being slaughtered for food. The boobies are also known as "clowns" because of their brightly colored feet and bills and bare face patches. The Red-footed booby, for example, has red feet, a blue bill and a blue face patch. The birds also make humorous grunts or shouts and whistling noises.

The Red-footed, Brown and White boobies are found in vast numbers. They nest throughout tropical and subtropical regions on islands in the Atlantic, Pacific and Indian oceans. Blue-footed boobies breed on the coasts and islands of western South America, in the Gulf of California and in the Galapagos Islands. They are noted for the way they often fish together in large groups, plunging simultaneously into the water. The Red-footed booby, especially, catches flying fish in the air.

▲ Unlike most of the other boobies, the Red-footed booby nests in bushes and low trees.

▼ Cape gannets live in southern Africa. The strip of naked black skin under the throat probably increases heat loss.

PUTTING ON A SHOW

All the gannets and boobies are territorial – they strongly defend their territory when nesting. This is very important, since most species nest in huge colonies extremely close to one another. The Peruvian booby nests in colonies of a million or more. In colonies of Cape gannets, there may be as many as six pairs to a square yard.

Gannets are particularly fierce fighters when establishing or defending their territory. Most of the other sulids instead indulge in some form of territorial display. This may involve shaking the head from side to side or bowing, with the wings spread out. Another common display is sky-pointing, in which a bird points its bill into the air as a signal to its mate.

Displays between the sexes are important in keeping pairs together. Birds often greet each other, after one has been away from the nest site, by stretching out their wings and banging their bills together. This is called mutual fencing. Boobies often do a dance during courtship to show off their brightly colored feet.

SURVIVAL OF THE STRONGEST

Most sulids nest on the ground or on cliff ledges, building simple nests of seaweed and other plant material. The Red-footed and Abbott's boobies, however, nest in trees, the former at low level, the latter high up. Both species lay only one egg. Like all the sulids, they incubate it under their webbed feet.

The gannets also almost always lay one egg. The Peruvian and Blue-footed boobies, however, regularly raise two or more young for they live in regions where there is usually plenty of food to feed them. The White and Brown boobies often lay two eggs, but a day or so after hatching one chick kills the other, ensuring that the stronger will survive.

Sulid chicks are born nearly naked and take from 3 to 5 months to

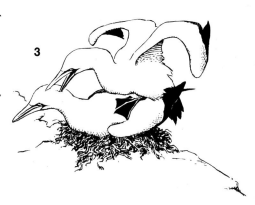

▲ Gannets and boobies perform displays to establish territory and during courtship. A male Brown booby (1) shakes its head to declare its territory. A pair of Atlantic gannets (2) fence with their bills as a gesture of greeting. The birds also display before mating (3).

▶ Blue-footed boobies nesting on desolate cliffs. Here, one bird flies in to replace its mate on the nest. By changing over regularly, both birds can feed as normal while continuing to incubate the eggs.

develop their flight feathers and begin to fly. They do not start to breed, usually in the colonies in which they were born, until they are 2 to 5 years old. Sulids live for about 20 years.

DWINDLING NUMBERS

The numbers of Peruvian boobies, which breed on the coasts and islands of Peru, can fluctuate widely. They

feed on the shoals of anchovies that normally teem in the cool surface waters offshore. These are the waters of the Humboldt current, which flows along western South America. They are rich in the plankton that the anchovies eat.

However, sometimes the current is disrupted by a flow of warm water known as El Niño. The plankton stay in the cooler deeper water, and the anchovies follow them, putting them out of reach of the boobies. When this happens the birds die by the million. Normally, when the cold current is restored, their numbers quickly recover. But this has not been happening in recent years, because of overfishing of the anchovy for human needs.

Even so, the Peruvian booby is not yet seriously at risk, unlike Abbott's booby. This species was once found widely on the islands of the western Indian Ocean. But over the years it has been driven by human activity from one island after another. Now it is found only on Christmas Island, and only about 1,500 breeding pairs remain. Even here it is under threat.

TROPICBIRDS

A group of tropicbirds circles over the cliffs of its tropical-island breeding site. These birds have just returned after months at sea. Wings held high and tail feathers flowing, they wheel and glide in unison. Their shrill, whistling calls fill the air. From time to time two birds veer away and begin flying together. Now and then one bird hovers over the other and touches it with the top of its tail feathers. Then the two swoop down, one leading the other to a nest hole in the cliff face. Courtship is over; it is time to mate and raise young.

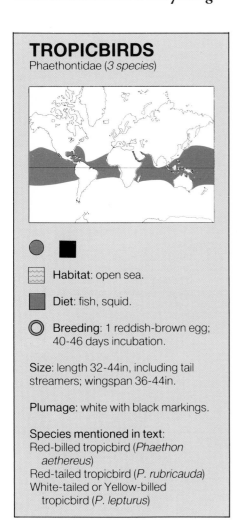

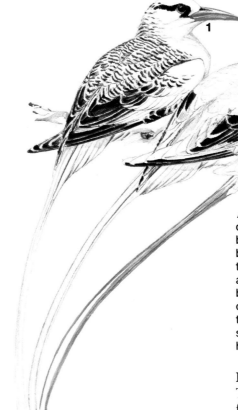

▲ The three species of tropicbird are distinguished by their different-colored bills and tails. The Red-billed tropicbird's bill (1) is always red, that of the White-tailed or Yellow-billed tropicbird (2) always yellow. The Red-tailed tropicbird's bill (3) is red when breeding, but otherwise yellow. The White-tailed tropicbird has white or yellow tail streamers, while the other two species have red or pink streamers.

Tropicbirds are found over tropical seas throughout the world. They return to land only in the breeding season. The White-tailed tropicbird, the smallest of the three species, is the most wide-ranging, being found in all tropical regions. The Red-billed tropicbird breeds in the Atlantic, eastern Pacific and north-western Indian oceans; the Red-tailed tropicbird in the western and central Pacific and the central and eastern Indian Oceans.

All three species of tropicbird have the distinctive streamers – long, thin feathers in the middle of the tail. This makes them easy to identify among the other sea-birds that they often nest with, such as frigatebirds and boobies. They also advertise their presence with their ear-piercing shrill call, which has been likened to the sound of a ship's bosun's whistle. For this reason they are often known as bosun birds.

HELPLESS ON LAND
Tropicbirds range widely in search of food, which is relatively scarce in tropical oceans. They take fish, particularly flying fish, and squid. Like their relatives the boobies and Brown pelican, they fish by plunge-diving from high in the sky. Folding back their wings, they dive into the water at high speed to make their catch. Their bodies are well-adapted for this, with large air sacs under the skin to absorb the shock of hitting the water.

Their plumage is waterproof, but they can dive only shallowly because their bodies are so buoyant (float easily). On land tropicbirds are nearly helpless. Their legs are so short and placed so far back on the body that all they can do is shuffle.

CLIFF OR GROUND NESTS
In some regions tropicbirds breed throughout the year, while in others breeding is seasonal. After a noisy aerial courtship display, pairs of birds search out their nest sites. Where possible, the birds nest in holes in the

▲The grace and beauty of a Red-tailed tropicbird. The two thin tail feathers, as long as the body, are held together, and the short webbed feet are tucked well in.

▼A Red-tailed tropicbird prepares to plunge-dive for fish.

cliffs. This gives them a convenient launch-pad for flying. They may also nest under rocks or bushes, even in scooped-out hollows in open ground. They often have to fight for a site with others of their species occupying the same colony.

GROWING UP

A female tropicbird lays only a single egg at a time, but a relatively large one for its body size. Both sexes help incubate the egg, taking shifts of up to 3 days each.

The chick, which hatches after about 6 weeks, is covered with thick down – unlike chicks of the tropicbird's relatives, which are born naked.

The down helps insulate the chick from the tropical heat. As a result, the parents are able to leave it alone after a day or so while they both go to catch fish to feed it. They feed it mouth to mouth, by regurgitating partly digested food. The chick is sometimes fed every day, but often only every 2 or 3 days.

It takes from 2 to 3 months, depending on how well it has been fed, for the young tropicbird to be strong enough to fly. As soon as it flies, feeding by the parents stops and the fledgling has to fend for itself. If it survives, it will not return to the nesting colony for 3 to 4 years and will start breeding when it is about 5 years old.

CORMORANTS

Ripples form on the still lake as the cormorant surfaces after a successful chase underwater. Dripping wet and with a fish wriggling in its bill, it flies off to a mooring post near by and swallows its catch. Then it unfolds its wings and stands with them outstretched, basking in the Sun.

CORMORANTS
Phalacrocoracidae and Anhingidae
(*33 species*)

● ■ 🐾

🌊 Habitat: inland waters and sea coast.

■ Diet: fish, water invertebrates.

◎ Breeding: cormorants: up to 6 bluish eggs, 22-26 days incubation; darters: up to 6 greenish eggs, 26-30 days incubation.

Size: cormorants: length 18-40in, wingspan 32-64in, weight 2-11lb; darters: length 30-40in, wingspan 48-51in, weight 2-5¾lb.

Plumage: cormorants: generally drab brown or black with a greenish sheen; darters: black or brown with varying amounts of white.

Species mentioned in text:
African darter (*Anhinga rufa*)
Common, Great or Black cormorant (*Phalacrocorax carbo*)
Galapagos flightless cormorant (*Nannopterum harrisi*)
Guanay or Peru cormorant (*Phalacrocorax bougainvillii*)
Shag (*P. aristotelis*)

Cormorants hold out their wings after diving to dry them off. This is necessary because, curiously for waterbirds, their feathers are not waterproof. However, water is able to penetrate the feathers quickly and drive out the air. This allows the birds to sink and dive easily.

Underwater, the wings of the cormorant are pressed tightly into the body to reduce drag. The completely webbed feet, powered by large thigh muscles, propel the bird swiftly as it chases fish. Cormorants may at times dive as deep as 165ft.

THE "SEA-CROW"
The word "cormorant" comes from French words meaning "sea-crow." Like the crow, the Common cormorant has dark plumage and is a very common bird. It is alternatively called the Great cormorant (North America)

and the Black cormorant (Australasia). The dark plumage of the bird is relieved only by white patches on the face and, in the breeding season, on the thighs.

Even darker is the shag, whose plumage is jet black all over with a glossy green sheen. It has a short head crest. While the Common cormorant is often found on inland waters as well, the shag is mainly a coastal bird.

Cormorants nest in vast colonies. The biggest ones are found on islands off the coast of Peru, where Peru cormorants or guanays nest in their millions. Like Peruvian boobies, they rely on the anchovies of the cold waters there for their existence. The presence of so many birds results in the islands becoming covered with thick layers of stinking, rotting waste. This waste, called guano, is removed and used as fertilizer.

▼The Spotted shag (*Phalacrocorax punctatus*) (1) and the Reed cormorant (*P. africanus*) (2) have head crests, particularly in the breeding season. The African darter (3) swims mostly submerged.

THE "SNAKE-BIRD"

Closely related to cormorants are four species of darter, also called anhingas after their family name, Anhingidae. They have a long neck with a long straight bill, together with long wings and tail, like a heron's. In the water they often swim like a snake, with only their neck above the surface. This gives them their popular name of "snake-bird."

When hunting, a darter stalks its prey slowly under the water, with its neck coiled. When a fish comes within range, it darts out its neck and stabs the fish in the side. A hinge mechanism in its neck bones allows it to dart and stab with lightning speed.

In South-east Asia, darters and cormorants are used for sport fishing. A ring placed round the neck stops the bird swallowing. When the bird surfaces, the fish is taken from its mouth.

▲After diving for fish, a Galapagos flightless cormorant holds out its wings to dry in the Sun.

▼African darters nesting in Lake Naivasha, Kenya. Darters prefer still waters and often colonize reservoirs.

FRIGATEBIRDS

A young frigatebird is out looking for food. It spies a booby flying home after a successful diving foray. It gives chase, and the booby is so frightened that it brings up the fish it has just swallowed. The young frigatebird immediately breaks off the attack and swoops down to snatch the fish out of the air.

Frigatebirds often rob other birds of their prey or nesting material by chasing them at high speed. This pirate-like behavior explains how they got their name as well as their alternative name of man-of-war bird.

Frigatebirds are easy to recognize in flight by their huge pointed wings and long forked tail. They have a slim body, and their tiny legs are so weak that they cannot walk. The toes of the feet are only slightly webbed, so the birds cannot swim. Also the plumage is not waterproof. Yet frigatebirds range far out to sea.

Their lack of swimming ability explains their method of fishing. They fly just above the surface, snap down the head and make a catch with their strong hooked bill. The birds pick up nesting material in the same way.

IN TROPICAL WATERS
Frigatebirds live only in the tropics. The Lesser and Great frigatebirds are found throughout most tropical parts,

of the world, but the other species are more restricted.

The Magnificent frigatebird ranges around both coasts of tropical America and the Caribbean. The Ascension Island species breeds only on that island in the Atlantic, and the Andrew's or Christmas Island frigatebird breeds only there, near Java in the Indian Ocean.

MAKING A SPECTACLE
Frigatebirds breed in colonies on small remote islands. Where possible, they nest in trees. Otherwise they have to nest on the ground.

During courtship, the males put on a group display to attract a mate. When females fly overhead, the males spread out and flutter their wings. They also throw back their head, inflate their scarlet throat pouch and call loudly or clack their bills.

When the male succeeds in attracting a female, it goes off to gather twigs and other material to build a nest. It

---

FRIGATEBIRDS
Fregatidae (*5 species*)

Habitat: open sea.

Diet: fish (mainly flying fish), squid.

Breeding: 1 chalky white egg; 44-55 days incubation.

Size: length 31-41in, wingspan 6½-7½ft, weight 1¾-3½lb; females heavier than males.

Plumage: males black with some white underneath; females black or dark brown and white.

Species mentioned in text:
Andrew's or Christmas Island
frigatebird (*Fregata andrewsi*)
Ascension Island frigatebird
(*F. aquila*)
Great frigatebird (*F. minor*)
Lesser frigatebird (*F. ariel*)
Magnificent frigatebird
(*F. magnificens*)

▼A pair of Great frigatebirds. The male inflates its conspicuous brilliant red throat pouch to attract a mate.

▶A Magnificent frigatebird about to land, with its pointed wings and long scissor-shaped tail outstretched.

takes this material on the wing or it steals twigs from other birds if it can. The female remains behind to build the nest and keep other birds away.

Both sexes help incubate the large single egg, taking shifts of up to 12 days each during incubation. The chick grows slowly and is fed by both parents by regurgitation even after it has learned to fly, maybe for a year.

Because frigatebirds take so long to raise their offspring, they probably breed only once every 2 years. They cannot use the same nest site, because it will have been taken over by another pair.

▶A male Lesser frigatebird catches a flying fish. It swoops down to the sea from high in the air, then snaps its bill down and back to pick up its prey.

HERONS AND BITTERNS

It is a day in early spring. The last Gray heron has returned to the heronry. Now the birds are gathered on open ground next to the nesting trees. Their bills and legs, usually yellow, have turned red with the onset of the breeding season. One by one the male birds fly up to the nests. They call loudly and point their bills in the air, trying to tempt females to join them. Eventually the female birds fly up and, with the males, build or repair the nests ready for egg-laying.

HERONS AND BITTERNS Ardeinae and Botaurinae (*60 species*)

⊖ ■ ♔

≋ **Habitat**: lakes, marshes, estuaries, coasts.

▦ **Diet**: fish, amphibians, small mammals, birds, insects.

○ **Breeding**: day and night herons: up to 7 white or bluish eggs; tiger herons: 1 or 2 whitish eggs, blotched red; 21-30 days incubation; bitterns: 3-6 olive-brown (large bitterns) or whitish green (small bitterns) eggs; 14-20 days incubation.

Size: herons: length 16-56in, weight up to 4½lb; bitterns: length 11-34in, weight up to 4lb.

Plumage: herons: varies widely, from all white, through mainly gray or blue, to chestnut-brown with contrasting stripes or patches; bitterns: mainly brown streaked with black.

Species mentioned in text:
Black-crowned night heron (*Nycticorax nycticorax*)
Black heron (*Egretta ardesiaca*)
Cattle egret (*Bubulcus ibis*)
Gray heron (*Ardea cinerea*)
Great blue heron (*A. herodius*)
Great white heron (*Egretta alba*)
Least bittern (*Ixobrychus exilis*)
Purple heron (*Ardea purpurea*)

Herons are long-legged and long-necked wading birds found in fresh-water habitats throughout the world. Only in far northern and Antarctic regions are they absent.

In flight herons can easily be recognized. They tuck in the neck, and the legs stretch far beyond the short tail. They beat their wings slowly, but can fly long distances. Northern populations migrate south in the winter.

Most herons develop a crest and plumes on the head, breast and back during the breeding season. They display this plumage during courtship and when defending their nest.

Herons have a number of areas of powder-down on their body. The down is made up of fine feathers that crumble into dust when rubbed with

◀**Size differences** The Great white heron **(1)** stands up to 3¼ft high. Like the Purple heron **(2)**, it is one of the day herons. Both the Lined or Tiger heron (*Tigrisoma lineatum*) **(3)** and the Yellow-crowned night heron (*Nyctanassa violaceae*) **(4)** usually feed at night.

▲Hunting for fish, a Black heron extends its wings over the water. Herons often do this, either to see better or to create a shadow to attract the fish.

▼When hunting, the Gray heron usually stands without moving in the water (1). When a fish swims by, the heron thrusts its head into the water with lightning speed to catch the fish (2). The heron kills the fish by banging it against hard ground (3). Then it washes the fish (4) before swallowing it head-first (5).

the bill. The birds apply the dust to their plumage when preening to clean it by absorbing fish oil and scum from the water.

VARIATIONS ON A THEME

The best-known species of heron are the day herons, which feed during the daytime. They include the common Gray heron, Great blue heron and Cattle egret.

The Gray heron ranges over a huge area, throughout Europe and much of Asia, and in Africa south of the Sahara. In western Europe this heron is mainly gray with a white neck and front. It has a black head crest and black markings on the neck. Farther east, the plumage becomes paler.

In North America there is a different species, very similar to the Gray heron, the Great blue heron. The Great white heron, though possibly a separate species, is probably an all-white form of the Gray or Great blue.

The Great white heron is also called the Great white egret, and in North America, the Common egret. The Cattle egret is a much smaller white heron, which spends much of its time among cattle on pastureland. The bird

feeds on insects the cattle stir up with their feet and also on ticks on the animals' hides.

BOOMING CALL
Several other species of heron feed mainly at night. They include the night herons, such as the Black-crowned night heron, which is found in Europe, Asia, Africa and the Americas. Night herons are short stocky birds, with large eyes. The tiger herons also feed at night. They get their name from their barred or striped plumage.

They are also frequently called tiger bitterns because they resemble bitterns in the following ways. First, when danger threatens, they thrust the bill in the air and stand very still. Their plumage provides good camouflage. Second, tiger herons have a distinctive booming call. And third, they are solitary creatures.

The true bitterns are stocky birds which spend all their time in the reeds. There are separate, but similar, species of large bittern in Africa, Eurasia and in the Americas. Eight species of small bittern are found throughout the world. Of these, the Least bittern of North America is the smallest of the heron family.

▼A pair of Purple herons with two young. These day herons feed and nest among the reeds in swampy habitats.

▶Motionless at the water's edge, a Gray heron waits for its prey. Its neck is coiled back ready to stab into the water.

STORKS

On the East African savannah vultures have gathered around the carcass of an antelope. They squabble as they tear at its flesh. Then two larger birds, with bald heads and large fleshy throat pouches, fly in. These are marabous. They harry the vultures and steal the food from their mouths.

Marabous, the largest of the storks, feed a lot on carrion. They also eat anything else around that is edible – eggs, young birds and mammals, insects and scraps. The adjutant storks of India and South-east Asia are closely related to the marabous and are also scavengers. Both marabou storks and adjutants have a bald head and a strong straight bill.

DIFFERENT FEEDING METHODS

The White and Black storks of southern Europe are more typical in their eating habits and in behavior. The White stork can often be seen walking slowly across the fields on its long legs, with its long neck stretched out and its head down looking for insects and worms. The Black stork tends to remain near the water, wading in the shallows to catch fish.

The wood storks, such as the American wood stork, also feed while wading. But they use touch rather than sight to locate their prey, just as spoonbills do. The open-bills, for

▲A threatening bill-clattering display (1). "Head-shaking crouch" performed by male as mate approaches (2). Part of an "up-down" courtship display (3).

▼Black stork (1), and Whale-headed stork (2), noted for its broad, hooked bill.

STORKS Ciconiidae, Scopidae, Balaenicipitidae (19 species)

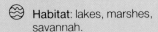

● ■ 𝅧

⊗ Habitat: lakes, marshes, savannah.

■ Diet: fish, insects, crustaceans, amphibians, small birds and mammals.

○ Breeding: 1-7 white or bluish eggs depending on species; 30-50 days incubation.

Size: length 30-60in; wingspan 5-10½ft; weight 4½-20lb.

Plumage: mainly white, gray and black; hammerhead, dark brown.

Species mentioned in text:
African open-bill stork (*Anastomus lamelligerus*)
American wood stork (*Mycteria americana*)
Black stork (*Ciconia nigra*)
Hammerhead (*Scopus umbretta*)
Marabou (*Leptoptilos crumeniferus*)
Whale-headed stork (*Balaeniceps rex*)
White stork (*Ciconia ciconia*)
Yellow-billed stork (*Ibis ibis*)

▲Gaping is one of the displays special to wood storks, like this Yellow-billed stork. Wood storks also have a bare head and a slightly down-curved bill.

▼White storks often nest on buildings, as here on a Spanish church.

instance the African open-bill stork, are touch-feeders too.

LONG-DISTANCE FLIGHT
On their long legs, storks walk with body upright and a purposeful stride. They can also run well. They fly powerfully with their long broad wings, the neck extended and feet straight out behind.

When flying, they usually alternate strong flapping flight with soaring on warm air currents. In this way they can travel long distances with ease while foraging and when migrating. The European White and Black storks migrate south each winter to southern Africa. There are also resident populations of these two species in Africa and eastern Asia.

GREETING DISPLAY
During courtship and nesting, storks put on some fascinating displays. Most common is the "up-down" display, performed as a greeting when one bird rejoins its mate on the nest. The birds raise and lower the head in a stiff characteristic way, clattering the bill at the same time. Some species may also whistle, hiss or scream.

Other interesting displays include, in wood storks, gaping and pretend preening. Male open-bills have an "advertising" display in which they lower the head between the legs and shift their weight from one foot to the other.

Nesting success depends on availability of food and on the weather; storks do not nest well in rainy areas.

IBISES AND SPOONBILLS

Night has fallen over the lake, and most birds have gone to roost. But a Roseate spoonbill is still splashing around in the shallows, looking for its supper. It has its bill open and shakes it from side to side under the water. Then something touches the sensitive inside of the bill, which snaps shut. The catch? A small wriggling fish.

IBISES AND SPOONBILLS
Threskiornithidae (*31 species*)

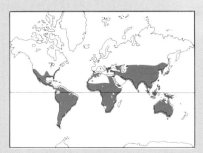 Habitat: lake shores, marshes, plains, savannah.

Diet: insects, crustaceans, carrion, fish.

Breeding: 2-5 white or bluish eggs; about 21 days incubation.

Size: length 19-43in; weight up to 9lb.

Plumage: white, brown, glossy black or pink.

Species mentioned in text:
African spoonbill (*Platalea alba*)
American white ibis (*Eudocimus albus*)
Bald ibis (*Geronticus calvus*)
European or White spoonbill (*Platalea leucorodia*)
Roseate spoonbill (*P. ajaia*)
Sacred ibis (*Threskiornis aethiopica*)
Scarlet ibis (*Eudocimus ruber*)

The Roseate spoonbill usually feeds by touch, which is why it can fish at night. All the ibises and spoonbills feed in this way. This means they can capture prey in muddy water and in thick underwater vegetation.

Spoonbills are so-called because of their long, flat bill, which broadens at the tip like a spoon. The Roseate species is the most colorful of them. As in other spoonbills, the head is bare. Mature birds have a tuft of pink plumes on the breast.

The Roseate spoonbill is a native of southern North America and South America, ranging from the Texas coast to Argentina. Other species of spoonbill are found in southern Europe, Asia, Africa and Australia. The European or White spoonbill is particularly widespread, ranging from southern and central Europe and North Africa to southern Asia. It is a large white bird with plumes of feathers on the nape of the neck.

DOWN-CURVED BILL

The swamps and marshes of North and South America are the home, not only for the Roseate spoonbill, but also for the even more colorful and well named Scarlet ibis. This bird is often found with the closely related American white ibis.

All the ibises have the same general build and a down-curved bill. Some species are noted for their naked head or plumes on the neck or body. The dark-colored Bald ibis of Africa and the Middle East has a bare head and neck plumes. The mainly white Sacred ibis has a bare black head and neck, with long dark plumes on its

▼ **Plumage** Ibises' plumage is often the same color all over: brown in the Glossy ibis (*Plegadis falcinellus*) **(1)**, white in the American white **(2)** and rare Japanese ibis (*Nipponia nippon*) **(3)**, and bright pink in the Scarlet ibis **(4)**. The Roseate spoonbill **(5)** has pink and white plumage.

back. It got its name because it was considered sacred in ancient Egypt. But it is no longer found in north-east Africa, breeding now south of the Sahara Desert.

SOCIABLE BIRDS

Ibises and spoonbills are very sociable birds, staying in flocks most of the time. They travel, feed, roost and nest together, not only with their own kind, but also with other wading birds, such as storks.

Most species nest in bushes, trees or reeds in rough nests of twigs and vegetation. The Bald ibis, which is found mainly in mountainous regions, nests on cliff ledges. Usually the male chooses the nest site and then displays with bill-pointing and bowing to attract a mate. Both sexes incubate the eggs and feed the young. The parents bring up partly digested food in the gullet, into which the young insert their bills to feed.

▲Vivid plumage makes these Scarlet ibises easy to see. Roosting with them are a few American white ibises.

▼A flock of African spoonbills. In flight, the birds extend the neck and trail their legs behind them.

FLAMINGOS

It is deafeningly noisy in the massive colony of Lesser flamingos nesting by an East African soda lake. The chicks have been hatched about a week and have so far stayed in the nest. But today, one after another, they are leaving the nest and gathering together in a nursery group, or crèche.

FLAMINGOS
Phoenicopteridae (*4 species*)

 Habitat: shallow salt or soda (alkaline) lagoons and lakes.

 Diet: algae, crustaceans, molluscs.

 Breeding: usually 1 white egg; 28 days incubation.

Size: length 32-58in, weight 2-6½lb; females smaller.

Plumage: pink or red, with black on wings.

Species mentioned in text:
Andean flamingo (*Phoenicoparrus andinus*)
Caribbean flamingo (*Phoenicopterus ruber ruber*)
Chilean flamingo (*P. r. chilensis*)
Greater flamingo (*P. r. roseus*)
James's flamingo (*Phoenicoparrus jamesi*)
Lesser flamingo (*Phoeniconaias minor*)

Flamingos are one of the easiest kinds of birds to recognize. All species, and sub-species, look much the same, differing only in size and slightly in coloring. They have a large body, with a long neck and long legs. Their plumage is pale pink to crimson, relieved by black on the outstretched wings. The bill and legs are either pink or yellow. The bill is bent in the middle, and the toes are fully and thickly webbed.

Flamingos are some of the most ancient species of bird. They were

▲A pair of Caribbean flamingos feeding. With its bright pink plumage, this species is the most colorful of all.

once widespread throughout Europe, North America and Australia, as well as in South America, Africa and India, where they are found now.

The Greater flamingo thrives in many places: in southern Europe, North and West Africa, southern Russia, India and South America. Lesser flamingos gather in greatest numbers around lakes in East Africa's Rift Valley. They are also found in

▼ "Wing saluting" displays by a Chilean flamingo (1) and a Greater flamingo (2). A Caribbean flamingo "twist-preens" (3). A Greater flamingo performs an inverted wing salute (4).

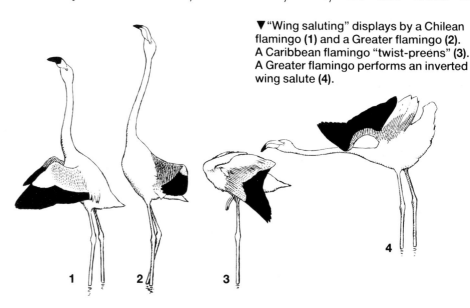

southern Africa and North-west India.

Other species are less widespread. The extremely colorful Caribbean flamingo is found in the West Indies, with a small colony in the Galapagos Islands in the Pacific. In South America the Andean flamingo stays mainly above 8,200ft up in the mountains. Above 11,500ft it lives with a much rarer species, James's flamingo.

UNIQUE FEEDERS

Flamingos are wading birds and use their feet to stir up the mud when feeding. They feed in a unique way, with the bill upside-down in the water. The upper jaw ("mandible") fits like a lid over the larger, trough-like lower jaw. The tongue is thick and covered in tiny spines.

Both jaws are fringed with tiny comb-like teeth ("lamellae"). When feeding, the flamingo takes water and mud into the bill. Then, with the bill upside-down, it pumps out the water through the lamellae, using its tongue as a piston. The lamellae filter out any small pieces of food.

Lesser flamingos feed mainly on the minute blue-green algae that thrive in the alkaline waters of Africa and India. The algae are a rich source of the pigment that tinges their plumage pink. The pigment is similar to that which gives carrots their color.

The larger Caribbean and Greater flamingos, on the other hand, tend to feed on larger prey, such as flies, shrimps and molluscs, which they take from the muddy bottom.

SPECTACULAR DISPLAYS

Flamingos live together in huge colonies. The birds feed together, nest together and display together. They perform one of the most spectacular group displays in the whole animal

▶ A Greater flamingo feeding its chick on "milk." This fluid is as nourishing as mammals' milk, but is colored bright red. Both sexes produce the milk.

world. A few birds begin to display first, but others around them soon join in until hundreds are performing together. There is usually a set pattern to the display, as though it had been carefully rehearsed. The movements known as "head-flagging" are usually followed by "wing-saluting" and by "twist-preening."

Normally the neck of the flamingo is held in an S-shape. But in head-

flagging the bird stretches up its neck stiffly, with the bill horizontal. In a wing salute, the bird spreads out its wings, then folds them again. This produces a flash of black against pink. In twist-preening the flamingo twists back its neck, drops a wing to expose the black feathers, and begins to preen behind the wing with its bill.

In another very impressive display flamingos quick-march together like soldiers on parade. They march back and forth, sometimes dipping the bill in the water as though feeding.

FLAMINGO "MILK"

Flamingos often perform group displays before nesting. In some way they help synchronize breeding – that is, make it happen at the same time for the whole colony. Both sexes build the nest. Using the bill, they scrape stones and mud into a circular mound beneath them. They also take turns to incubate the single egg and, after hatching, to feed the chick. When it is a few days old, the chick leaves the nest and joins hundreds of other chicks in a nursery group or crèche.

When first hatched, flamingo chicks have a covering of gray down, a straight, pink bill, and pink legs. But after about a week, the bill and/or legs take on the adult colors. The first plumage is also gray. Adult plumage does not appear for 2 to 3 years.

The adult birds feed their offspring on "milk," a fluid produced in the crop. Pigeons are the only other birds that do this. Most flamingo species carry on feeding until the young birds begin to fly. By then the bill is fully bent and equipped for filter-feeding.

HUMAN THREAT

Breeding is usually successful since flamingos have few natural enemies. This is because their favorite habitat is alkaline waters, which support little in the way of vegetation.

Human beings pose the greatest threat to flamingos by disturbing or destroying their habitats. Many desirable habitats have been spoilt by mining activities, for example. Capturing these very attractive birds for zoos and wildlife parks also reduces their number. Many birds have died from stress as a result of their contact with people.

▲ Flamingos gather in huge colonies, and are a beautiful sight when they take to the air together. These are Chilean flamingos feeding in a lake 13,200ft up in the Andes mountains.

▶ These Greater flamingos are "head-flagging" at the beginning of a group display. They hold the neck straight up, with the bill horizontal like a flag.

▼ A group of Lesser flamingos filter feeding in the water. This flamingo species, the smallest, has a much darker bill than the others.

SWANS AND GEESE

A family of Mute swans is swimming sedately among the reeds in a still backwater. In front is the male, ever on the lookout for danger. The female follows, one cygnet on its back, four more swimming behind. As the male comes out of the reeds, it spies a rival male close by. Arching its wings and drawing in its neck, it surges towards the intruder at high speed. The rival takes fright and flees. The proud father rears out of the water and flaps its wings in triumph.

▼ Snow geese in their thousands gather to feed. Within the flock, family groups usually stay together.

SWANS AND GEESE
Anatidae (tribes Anserini, Anser-anatini) and Anhimidae (*25 species*)

≈ **Habitat:** sea coasts, estuaries, lakes, rivers.

◰ **Diet:** fish, molluscs, crustaceans, insects, vegetation.

◎ **Breeding:** 4-14 white, bluish or greenish eggs; 18-39 days incubation.

Size: length up to 5ft; weight up to 33lb; wingspan up to 6½ft (Mute swan).

Plumage: often white or black and white; also gray, brown.

Species mentioned in text:
Barnacle goose (*Branta leucopsis*)
Bewick's or Whistling swan (*Cygnus columbianus*)
Black swan (*C. atrata*)
Black-necked swan (*C. melanchoryphus*)
Canada goose (*Branta canadiensis*)
Emperor goose (*Anser canagicus*)
Magpie goose (*Anseranas semipalmata*)
Mute swan (*Cygnus olor*)
Pink-footed goose (*Anser fabalis brachyrhyncus*)
Red-breasted goose (*Branta ruficollis*)
Snow goose (*Anser caerulescens*)
Trumpeter swan (*Cygnus buccinator*)
Whooper swan (*C. cygnus*)

Mute swans are naturally quarrelsome and become extremely aggressive in the breeding season when they are defending their territory. They are powerful creatures, which by flapping their wings hard can inflict severe injuries on any humans who disturb them. They are the largest of the swans, easily recognizable by their graceful curved neck, their orange bill and the knob at the base of the bill.

WHITE AND BLACK SWANS

The plumage of the Mute swan is all white. So is that of the other swans in the Northern Hemisphere. These include the Whooper and Bewick's swans. The Whooper is almost as large as the Mute swan, but can be distinguished by its straight neck and by its bill, which is black and yellow. Bewick's swan is similar, but rather smaller, with less yellow on the bill.

▲A male Canada goose races up to a rival and threatens with an aggressive mouth-open display.

▼A male Black swan incubating on the nest. It shares this chore with the female, which is unusual among swans.

Both species are noisier than the Mute swan. The Whooper swan has a trumpeting call, like the even louder Trumpeter swan, which is another northern species. The Mute swan is noisier in flight, however. Its slow wing beats produce an unmistakable wheezy, buzzing sound.

Two of the most distinctive swans live in the Southern Hemisphere. The Black swan of Australia is all black with a red bill. The Black-necked swan of South America has a black head and neck, which contrast with its otherwise white plumage. There is a red knob on its blue bill, and its feet are pink. A white stripe around its eyes and head is only sometimes distinct.

BIRDS OF THE NORTH

The 15 species of geese are found only in the Northern Hemisphere. Geese show a much wider variation in plumage than swans. One of the most colorful is the Red-breasted goose of Siberia, which has black, white and chestnut-red markings. It is one of the black geese, so-called for their generally dark plumage. They belong to the *Branta* genus. Other black geese include the quite similar Barnacle and Canada geese, which have a black head and neck and pale breast. The Barnacle goose has a white face, and the Canada goose a white chin patch. The Barnacle can be identified by its yapping call, like that of a small dog.

▼Species of swan and goose and some aspects of their behavior Bar-headed goose (*Anser indicus*) (1). Aggressive posture of the Red-breasted goose (2). Magpie goose (3). Crested screamer (*Chauna torquata*) (4). Triumph displays of male Hawaiian goose (*Branta sandvicensis*) (5) and Whooper swan (6). Emperor goose nesting on the tundra (7). Pink-footed goose (8). Black-necked swan and cygnets (9).

1

4

5

8

9

RG

The paler-colored gray geese belong to the *Anser* genus. They include the Emperor goose and the Pink-footed goose. Palest is the beautiful Snow goose. Its plumage is all white, except for the wing tips, and it has a red bill and pink legs.

GOOSE STEP

Swans and geese are well adapted for their life on or near water. The body is well insulated, and the plumage is waterproof. The legs are powerful, and the toes webbed for swimming.

The bill of swans and geese is quite broad and is usually open at the sides, where there are fine comb-like "teeth" ("lamellae"). These are used to help filter food particles from the water. But geese in particular also feed by grazing at water margins and on pastureland.

Swans are more aquatic than geese. Their legs are short and placed well back on the body. They cannot walk well on land. Geese, with longer legs placed further forward, are able to walk readily and even run quite fast. Some walk lifting their feet high, with an exaggerated "goose step."

MAGPIES AND SCREAMERS

The Magpie goose of Australasia has especially long legs. Its toes are only slightly webbed. Unusually for a goose, it often perches in trees.

Screamers (family Anhimidae) are other birds related to, but different from, true geese. Like the Magpie goose they have scarcely any webbing on their long toes. They have a short hooked bill. All three species of screamer, which live in South America, are noted for their loud penetrating call. Their "scream" is different from the "honking" of true geese.

PAIRED FOR LIFE

The male and female in a pair of swans or geese usually remain together for life. They often preen each other and display together. These activities help cement their relationship. One typical display is the "triumph ceremony," performed when they have driven away an intruder. Waving the head and lifting the wings, they call loudly as if to say, "Let that be a lesson!"

Swans and geese usually nest away from other birds, sometimes defending a wide territory around the nest. In most cases only the female builds the nest and incubates the eggs. She builds the nest from plant material and usually lines it with down from her breast. She covers up the eggs with the down when leaving the eggs to feed.

Both sexes feed and look after the chicks when they hatch, remaining with them throughout the first winter. The juveniles have different plumage from the adults. Young Mute swans, for example, look ordinary ("ugly ducklings") in their dull-brownish plumage, until suddenly they grow into graceful adulthood.

Many swans and geese breed in far northern regions – in Greenland, Siberia and Arctic North America. They migrate south to spend winter in warmer climates every year, flying in typical V-formations, or skeins. They return to their breeding grounds in the spring as the snows clear. Their annual migrations are one of the great rhythms of nature, marking the passage of the seasons.

A LEADEN DEATH

Swans and geese are, with ducks, classed as waterfowl. They have been hunted for thousands of years for their eggs, meat and plumage, and more recently for sport. Few species are as yet under threat from shooting. But many birds die as an indirect result of it, from lead poisoning by shotgun pellets they pick up from the ground. Others suffer lead poisoning from swallowing the lead weights carelessly dropped by anglers.

▶The beautiful Mute swan thrashing its wings in the water to bathe its plumage.

DUCKS

After fishing on the lake, a female goosander flies up to a tree near the water's edge. It perches near a hole, where several fluffy little heads soon appear. The female flies down to the ground and calls to its young, which are only a few days old. After some hesitation the ducklings jump down from the tree. They land in a heap, but unharmed. Then they follow their mother to the water's edge.

Ducks are among the most widespread and the most colorful of all waterfowl. They are found on all the continents except Antarctica. Many species are shot for sport, while others such as the mergansers are killed by anglers because they take fish.

Ducks are mostly quite small birds, with a short neck and short legs. The body is well adapted for life on the

water. The breast is broad and flat, like a boat-bottom. The plumage is waterproof, and the feet are webbed. The legs are set well back on the body to aid swimming. But this makes walking on land awkward, resulting in the typical duck waddle.

Ducks belong, with the swans and geese (see pages 48-53), to the family Anatidae. They are generally classified

◄When diving, the Tufted duck (1) holds its wings close to the body; the White-winged scoter (2) has its slightly open.

into different tribes according to their body structure, plumage or behavior. The tribes are whistling ducks (9 species), Freckled duck (1), shelduck and sheldgeese (16), steamer ducks (3), perching ducks and geese (13), dabbling ducks (40), diving ducks (16), sea ducks and sawbills (20) and stifftails (8).

COLORFUL MALES

In most species the male (drake) is more highly colored. The female (duck) is generally a dull brown. This inconspicuous coloring acts as camouflage when the duck is sitting on the nest incubating the eggs.

When molting, the drake sheds its flight feathers and cannot fly for several weeks. During this time it goes into "eclipse plumage," which is dull

▼►Variation in plumage The attractive Mandarin (1) is a perching duck. The White-faced tree duck (*Dendrocygna viduata*) (2), a whistling duck, also perches in trees. The Red-breasted merganser (3) is a sawbill, the Ruddy duck (4) a stifftail.

DUCKS Anatidae (9 tribes)
(*126 species*)

⊛ Habitat: freshwater wetlands, estuaries, coasts.

◪ Diet: water weed, seeds, insects, molluscs, frogs, small fish.

◯ Breeding: 6-14 whitish, creamy, bluish or greenish eggs; 3-4 weeks incubation.

Size: length 14-28in; weight up to 4½lb.

Plumage: highly variable in males: mixtures of black, white, brown, chestnut red; usually speckled dull brown in females.

Species mentioned in text:
Black scoter (*Melanitta nigra*)
Common eider (*Somateria mollissima*)
Common or European pochard (*Aythya ferina*)
Freckled duck (*Stictonetta naevosa*)
Goosander or Common merganser (*Mergus merganser*)
Mallard (*Anas platyrhynchos*)
Mandarin duck (*Aix galericulata*)
North American wood duck (*A. sponsa*)
Pintail (*Anas acuta*)
Red-breasted merganser (*Mergus serrator*)
Redhead (*Aythya americana*)
Ruddy duck (*Oxyura jamaicensis*)
Shelduck (*Tadorna tadorna*)
Shoveler (*Anas clypeata*)
Teal (*A. crecca*)
Tufted duck (*Aythya fuligula*)
White-winged scoter (*Melanitta fusca*)

▶ The Black-headed duck (*Heteronetta atricapilla*) of South America is a parasite when it comes to nesting. It lays its eggs in the nests of other waterfowl.

brown just like that of the female, for camouflage.

(Except where otherwise stated, the plumage colors mentioned for the different species of duck described below refer to the male.)

THE DABBLERS

Many species of duck feed at the surface by dabbling – constantly dipping the bill into the water and sifting out bits of food. Their bills are edged with lamellae (comb-like teeth) which act like a sieve. Dabbling ducks often up-end themselves for a few seconds to reach weed underwater.

Some of the most common species of ducks are dabblers. They include

the mallard, teal, pintail and shoveler. All these species are widespread and are found right across northern North America and Eurasia.

The mallard can be found on virtually any small pond in the town as well as in the country. It has a dark green head, is maroon on the breast, and has a yellow bill.

The smaller teal has a handsome head of chestnut red, with a glossy dark green eye patch. A patch of yellow beneath the tail shows up in flight. When alarmed, teals take off almost vertically. They fly in tightly bunched flocks.

▼ **Four distinctive species of duck**
Males are shown. The shelduck (1) is heavy-bodied like a goose. Unusually in ducks, the female has similar plumage. But it lacks the knob on the bill. The pintail (2) has an unmistakable tail, an elegant body and long wings. The Common eider (3) has a much plumper body shape. The Tufted duck (4) has a noticeably rounded, purplish black head with a long tuft of feathers on the nape.

The pintail is easy to recognize because of its long, sharply pointed tail. The shoveler's most distinctive feature is its long bill, which broadens at the tip like a shovel.

THE DIVERS

The tribe of diving ducks generally live in freshwater habitats. When diving, they usually keep the wings tight into the body. But some species use the wings to help them steer underwater.

The diving ducks are often called bay ducks or pochards. The Common or European pochard is gray and black with a chestnut-red head. The redhead of North America is similar, but is larger and darker. The scaups are also related and are probably named for their habit of diving for scallops. They often feed along the sea coast.

Stifftails are also very good divers. These small dumpy birds are named after their long spiky tail feathers, which they use for steering underwater. They usually have a chestnut-red plumage, often with a black-and-white head. The Ruddy duck is typical. It lives in North America, unlike most stifftails, which live in the Southern Hemisphere.

1

2

▼ Fluffy-feathered mallard ducklings dabble among the duckweed. They scoop up a mouthful of water, then strain out from it seeds, leaves and insects.

SEA DUCKS AND SAWBILLS

Some species of diving duck spend much of their time at sea. A well-known example of these sea ducks is the Common eider. The soft down that the female plucks from its breast during nesting has been gathered for centuries to make eiderdown quilts. The eider is a striking bird, with black belly and flight feathers and black cap; the rest of the plumage is white, with tinges of pink on the breast and green on the nape. It breeds in far northern regions, like another very distinctive sea duck, the Black scoter. This bird is black all over, except for an orange mark on the bill.

The sawbills are close relatives of the sea ducks, but they are usually found on inland waters. They get their name from the saw-tooth edge to their bill, which helps them grasp the fish they catch when they dive. This group includes the mergansers.

GOOSE-LIKE DUCKS

In the United States mergansers are sometimes called sheldrakes. This can cause confusion with the quite different shelduck and sheldgeese. The shelduck is a northern coastal and inland bird with a goose-like body. Sheldgeese are similar in build.

The steamers of southern South America and the Falkland Islands are sometimes classified with shelducks and like them are heavily built. The group name comes from their habit of thrashing their wings like a paddle-steamer when racing over water. Two of the three species are flightless.

WHISTLING IN THE TREES

Most ducks spend their time on the water or on ground close by. A few species, however, have the habit of perching in trees. Among the most attractive of them are the Mandarin duck of Asia and the North Amer-ican wood duck. Most tree-perching species are found in the tropics.

The birds usually nest in hollows in trees. The young have sharp claws and a stiff tail to help them climb out of the nest hole a few days after hatching. A few other ducks nest in trees, including the goosander.

The whistling ducks are another tribe of ducks that often perch in trees. Also called tree ducks, they are found mainly in tropical and subtropical regions in the Americas, Africa and Asia. They are noted for their high-pitched whistling call. Both sexes have similar plumage, which is usually highly patterned.

NESTING AND BREEDING

During courtship, drakes put on displays to attract the females and prepare them for mating. They may jerk back the head and make whistling noises, flick water with the bill or splash with the feet, cock the tail or even "burp."

Most ducks build nests on the ground or in reed beds, with grass, weed, leaves and feathers. Exceptions are the perching ducks and goosander, which are tree-nesters, and the shelduck, which nests in burrows. Most ducks nest away from other birds, though some do nest close together if space is limited.

Only the female builds the nest and incubates the eggs. Incubation begins when the whole clutch is laid, and the young hatch within a few hours of one another. They have their eyes open and are covered in thick soft down. After only a few hours in the nest drying off, they are ready to follow their mother into the water and start to swim. Among sea ducks and shelducks several broods often join up to form a nursery group or crèche under the care of a few females.

A pair of ducks usually stay together for only one season. This happens because, after mating, the drake takes little or no part in raising the young.

CRANES

A flock of cranes is quietly preening. Then, for no reason at all, a pair of birds becomes agitated and begin to dance. They bow to one another in a courtly manner and start bouncing and leaping high into the air with wings out-stretched. The exuberance of their dance is infectious and tempts other pairs near by to join in. Within a short while the whole flock gets in the dancing mood and is prancing about madly. The air is filled with the cranes' deafening bugle-like calls.

Cranes are among the most graceful birds on Earth. They are long-legged and long-necked and have an elegant, upright stance. Some species stand nearly 6½ft tall, which makes them the world's tallest flying birds. Their wingspan can exceed 6½ft.

WETLAND BIRDS

Cranes are mainly wetland birds, but their feet are not webbed. They spend most of their time in the shallows where they feed and rest at night. The crowned cranes are unusual because they roost in trees.

Except for the Arctic, the Antarctic and South America, cranes can be found throughout the world. In South America their place is taken by a relative, the limpkin.

The Common crane of northern Europe and Asia has mainly gray plumage with black flight feathers on the wings. Its neck is striped black and white, and it has a patch of red skin on the head. It migrates south during the winter to the south of Spain and Portugal, North Africa and India.

Other northern species fly south in winter, including the rare Siberian crane and the Whooping crane of North America. These cranes also

CRANES Gruidae, Aramidae (*16 species*)	

eggs, 28-36 days incubation; limpkin: 4-8 speckled eggs, 20 days incubation.

Size: cranes: height 3-6ft, weight 6-23lb; limpkin: length 24-28in, weight 2-3lb.

Plumage: mainly white or gray.

Species mentioned in text:
Black-crowned crane (*Balearica pavonina*)
Blue or Stanley crane (*Anthropoides paradisea*)
Common crane (*Grus grus*)
Demoiselle crane (*Anthropoides virgo*)
Limpkin (*Aramus guarauna*)
Siberian crane (*Bugeranus leucogeranus*)
Whooping crane (*Grus americana*)

⊛ **Habitat:** swamp, grassland.

◨ **Diet:** insects, fish, snails, seeds.

◯ **Breeding:** cranes: 1-3 speckled

▼The limpkin (1) is named after its curious slow gait, which makes it look as if it is limping. The handsome Demoiselle crane (2), a northern relative of the Blue crane, is noted for the tuft of feathers on its neck and the plumes on its chest.

▶When cranes dance, they go through a complicated sequence of steps and actions. During dancing the birds frequently bob and bow (1). They also perform leaps and may toss stones, sticks or feathers into the air (2). Often one bird leaps while the other bows (3). When face to face, the dancing may transform into stiff threat postures of stamping and wing-flapping (4).

▼Blue cranes, also called Stanley cranes, are named for their bluish-gray plumage. Like Demoiselle cranes, they have ornamental head and breast feathers and a relatively short bill.

have the bare red face patch that is typical of all species of the *Grus* genus.

The most distinctive of all cranes is the Black-crowned crane of Africa. It has a dark body with white and reddish-brown on the wings. Its head is magnificent, black with white ear patches, a red throat patch and a large fan-shaped "crown" of light orange-brown feathers on top.

Cranes have a shrill call which in some species sounds very much like a bugle. It can carry for several miles The reason they can call so loudly is because of their long windpipe, which is coiled in their breast like a French horn. In the Whooping crane the windpipe is as much as 5ft long and gives rise to the loud call for which the bird is named.

THREATENED CRANES

The Whooping crane is the rarest of the cranes. Only about 100 birds are thought to remain in the wild, and about half this number in captivity. Whooping cranes breed in Canada's North-West territories, flying south to Texas for the winter. Under total protection, their numbers are recovering, but slowly because they have a low breeding rate. Other species of crane are also under threat, some because of illegal hunting, but most because of the drainage of wetlands.

WAKE-UP CALLS

A mating pair of cranes often maintains a wide territory, which they announce at dawn with a loud unison call. This is a duet, in which long low calls from the male blend with shorter high-pitched calls from the female.

Both male and female build the nest and share the incubation of the eggs. The chicks are hatched well developed and covered in down. They can swim and walk after a few hours.

▶ Black crowned cranes flying over the savannah in East Africa. Their neck is stretched out in front, their long legs extended straight behind.

RAILS

A flock of coots is feeding in the shallows of a flooded gravel pit. They dive to the bottom to reach the weed, returning to the surface to eat it. But some of the birds craftily wait for others to return from a dive and then steal the weed from them.

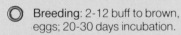
Coots are among the most familiar of the groups of birds belonging to the rail family. The other groups include the gallinules, the crakes and the rails themselves. The rails are one of the most widespread of all bird families, living in mainly wetland habitats in most parts of the world except the Arctic and Antarctic.

Rails have short wings and are usually not strong fliers; some species are flightless. But their legs are strong, and they run well. They have long toes, which in some species are equipped with fleshy lobes. This helps the birds walk easily on vegetation.

THE BALD COOT
Coots have a sooty black plumage all over, which contrasts with a white bill and naked patch on the forehead. This patch, called a frontal shield, makes the bird look as though it is going bald. This explains the expression "bald as a coot," used to describe bald people.

The European coot and the American coot, or mudhen, are very similar and very common. The larger Giant

▲ The Water rail is an athletic bird which can leap as high as 3ft out of the water to catch insects such as dragonflies.

▼ A family of European coots on the nest, a mound of vegetation built among plants in the shallows.

and Horned coots are much rarer and confined to lakes high in the Andes mountains of South America.

PLAIN AND GAUDY

The commonest of the gallinules, which is often found in the same areas as coots, is the moorhen. Also called the Common gallinule, it is found throughout Europe, Africa and North America. It is slightly smaller than the coot, but easily distinguished from the coot because of its bright red frontal shield. It also has a white under-tail, which it flashes in displays.

In comparison, the Purple gallinule is gaudy, with a stunning plumage of turquoise and emerald green and a blue shield. It ranges from the southern United States south to Argentina. A similarly colorful species is found in the Mediterranean, and another related bird lives in Africa.

The takahe of New Zealand is also very colorful, with a broad red bill and frontal shield. It is the biggest of the rails, flightless and extremely rare.

ELUSIVE BIRDS

The crakes have speckled brown plumage and short bills; some look rather like partridges. The Spotted crake is found widely in Europe and Asia, but like most crakes is a secretive bird which is not often seen. Its equivalent in North America is the sora or Carolina rail. The Eurasian corncrake is also an elusive bird. It is seldom seen, but can be detected by its rasping call, which sounds like a knife being scraped over the teeth of a comb.

The long-billed rails, such as the brown and gray Water rail, are also more often heard than seen. They have a call that has been likened to that of a young pig squealing. Several long-billed rails are flightless. Most of these are now rare as a result of habitat destruction. But the New Guinea flightless rail, big and strong enough to eat rats, still thrives.

▲The Purple gallinule (1) is the most colorful member of the rail family. Its toes are long to help it walk easily over floating vegetation. The Crested coot (2) has also two red knobs on the forehead.

▼A pair of Black crakes walking on lily-pads in a lake in East Africa. Their toes are long and well splayed to distribute the weight over as large an area as possible.

PLOVERS

PLOVERS Charadriidae
(62 species)

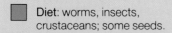 **Habitat:** mainly marsh, estuary, rivers, grassland.

Diet: worms, insects, crustaceans; some seeds.

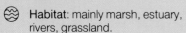 **Breeding:** 2-4 brown-speckled eggs; 18-38 days incubation.

Size: length 5½-16½in; weight 1-10 ounces.

Plumage: brown, often speckled or greenish-black on top, pale below.

Species mentioned in text:
Australian banded plover (*Vanellus tricolor*)
Black-fronted plover (*Charadrius melanops*)
Gray or Black-bellied plover (*Pluvialis squatarola*)
Greater golden plover (*P. apricaria*)
Killdeer (*Charadrius vociferus*)
Lapwing or peewit (*Vanellus vanellus*)
Lesser golden plover (*Pluvialis dominica*)
Little ringed plover (*Charadrius dubius*)
Ringed plover (*C. hiaticula*)
Spur-winged plover (*Vanellus spinosus*)
Wattled plover (*V. senegallus*)
Wrybill (*Anarhynchus frontalis*)

▶ The Black-fronted plover of Australia nests in a bare scrape in the ground. The speckled brown plumage of the back wings and head provide good camouflage when the bird is on the nest incubating the eggs. The spotted brown eggs are even better camouflaged.

A fox is hunting on the beach. As it begins moving in the direction of a plover and its chicks, the plover gets up and runs away. Then it squats down, flapping a wing as if injured. The fox senses a quick kill and chases after it, but the plover flies away. By luring away the fox, the bird has saved the chicks.

The plovers are among the most successful of all bird families. They can be found throughout the world, except for a few desert regions and the permanently frozen Arctic and Antarctic. They are plumpish birds with a round head. They are classed as waders, and most do nest and feed in water margins along coasts, estuaries and inland waters. Many can also be found well away from water on grasslands and farm fields.

Unlike most other waders, plovers have a short bill, which is rather like that of a pigeon. In all except one species the bill is straight. The exception is the wrybill from New Zealand, which has its bill bent to the right at an angle of more than 10 degrees. No other bird in the world has a beak with such a marked sideways curve.

The legs of plovers are quite long and sturdy and enable them to run fast. Most plovers have only three forward-facing toes; the hind toe is absent. The toes are not webbed.

The eyes of plovers are relatively large, and the birds feed mainly by sight, usually in damp areas and at the water's edge. Typically when they feed, they run in short bursts, darting at prey they have spied. They often patter their feet on the ground to bring prey to the surface.

THE TRUE PLOVERS
The birds called true plovers or sandplovers belong to the genus *Charadrius*. They are the smallest plovers. Among the 30 or so species are the Ringed plover and the similarly marked, but smaller, Little ringed plover of Eurasia. Both have a black and white ring on the neck and black and white

markings on the head. The larger bird can be distinguished by the orange upper bill and the orange legs.

The Ringed plover breeds around the coasts of the British Isles, Scandinavia and the extreme north of Europe and Asia, as well as in Greenland. The Little ringed plover is found throughout Europe and Asia except in the extreme north. Most birds fly south to winter along the eastern Mediterranean or in Africa.

The killdeer is the commonest true plover in North America. It also ranges into north-west South America. It has broadly similar markings to the ringed plovers, but has two neck rings, not one. It is named after the sound of its loud whistle. The northern populations of the killdeer fly south to escape the winter snows, but return almost as soon as the snow has melted.

THE LAPWINGS

The larger plovers of the genus *Vanellus* are referred to as lapwings. They are found in temperate and tropical regions throughout the world except for North America. Some members of the 20 or so lapwing species boast a crest, face wattles and a spur on the wing. These appendages usually feature in the breeding displays of the birds.

The most familiar crested bird is the common lapwing of Eurasia. It is also known as the peewit after its plaintive call. In winter large flocks of lapwings migrate south to warmer

▼The gold speckles on its plumage give the Greater golden plover (1) its name. The killdeer (2) has black and white bands on its face and neck. It is shown here in its "broken wing" position. The Wattled plover (3) has wattles on the face and spurs on its wings.

65

climates. The wattles and spur are well displayed by the Wattled plover of southern Africa.

LONG-DISTANT MIGRANTS
The largest birds of the plover family are three species belonging to the *Pluvialis* genus. With a body length of nearly 12in, they are almost twice as big as the ringed plovers. They breed in northern regions of the Northern Hemisphere, as far up as the Arctic tundra.

The Greater golden plover has gold-speckled plumage and, in the breeding season, a coal-black face, breast and belly. The far northern populations migrate early in winter to Britain, south-west Europe and north-west Africa.

In Siberia and North America the species is replaced by the similar Lesser golden plover. This bird migrates for the winter over very long distances indeed. From the Arctic, some populations fly across the Atlantic to Argentina and across the Pacific to Australia.

The Gray or Black-bellied plover is another striking bird in its summer plumage. The upper parts are a speckled dark gray; the face, breast and belly are black. The black turns to light gray in winter. The Gray plover breeds on the Arctic tundra and migrates south in winter, sometimes as far as to Chile in South America and to Australia.

DISPLAYING AND BREEDING
Most plovers display early in the breeding season to prepare for mating and nest building and to declare their territory. On the ground, displaying birds bow and curtsy, spread their wings, fan the tail and call loudly. The most spectacular of these performances is the aerial display of the lapwing. It climbs into the air with slow wingbeats and then goes into a twisting, tumbling dive almost to the ground, ending with a flurry of rapid wingbeats before it lands.

Some pairs of plovers nest in colonies along with several hundred other pairs. But most nest by themselves and hold quite a large territory, especially where food is limited.

The nests are simple scrapes in the ground, usually made by the male, using its breast. It makes several scrapes, from which the female then chooses one in which to lay the eggs.

▲ The tumbling flight of lapwings (1). A pair of golden plovers fight a "song duel" (2). One Spur-winged plover in threat posture (3); another runs at a rival (4).

▶ An Australian banded plover spreads its wings and gives an alarm call to challenge an intruder.

▼ The common lapwing can be seen on farmland throughout Europe and Asia.

Usually four eggs are laid and are incubated by both male and female. As many as three clutches may be laid in a season, although one is normal in colder climates.

PROTECTING THE NEST
The eggs and the nesting birds are well camouflaged, which is essential because the nests are always out in the open. They are difficult to detect even from a few feet away.

If a predator or an intruder gets too close and poses a threat to the eggs, nesting birds switch to another defense. They run off and feign injury with a "broken wing" display to lead the unwanted visitor away from the nest (and later, once the chicks have hatched, from them too).

Plover chicks hatch fully developed, and they are able to run within an hour. Their brown and white speckled downy plumage provides them with perfect camouflage against predators. They freeze instantly when the parents give their alarm call.

SANDPIPERS

It is spring, and a Common snipe is showing off. It climbs up to 100ft on rapid wingbeats. Then, fanning out the tail, it goes into a shallow dive. As the air rushes past, it vibrates the outer tail feathers, producing a drumming noise.

The Common snipe is a member of the sandpiper family of waders. These birds breed mainly in the Northern Hemisphere, particularly in the Arctic and sub-Arctic. But they range widely as they migrate south in winter to southern Europe, Africa, South America and Australia.

The coasts and estuaries of the British Isles are among the world's most important wintering grounds for sandpipers, particularly dunlin and knot. The winter plumage of many sandpipers is grayish. In summer the birds develop camouflage plumage of mottled brown. This is necessary because they nest on the ground and need to be protected when incubating the eggs.

HARD TO DISTINGUISH

In their mainly gray winter plumage, it is often difficult to tell one sandpiper from another. They can sometimes be distinguished by their bill shape, size or color, or by the color of their legs. The dunlin has a thick black, slightly down-curved bill and black legs. The similar sized Common sandpiper has a much thinner, paler and straight bill and greenish legs. The Green sandpiper looks much the same. But it is unusual because it nests, not on the ground, but in abandoned birds' nests.

Many species have long bills for probing into the sand and mud for worms and shellfish. The shorter-billed species feed at the surface. The

▼ The Common snipe (1) in flight shows the separated tail feathers that make a distinctive drumming sound. The redshank (2), is named after its bright colored legs. The sanderling (3) scurries back and forth at the edge of the waves when feeding.

SANDPIPERS
Scolopacidae (*81 species*)

⬡ ■ ✦

✺ **Habitat:** wetlands, grasslands, estuaries, coasts.

■ **Diet:** molluscs, crustaceans, worms, insects; some plant material.

◯ **Breeding:** 2-4 buff or greenish, often brown-speckled eggs; 18-30 days incubation.

Size: length 5-27in; weight ⅔ ounce-2¼lb.

Plumage: upper parts mottled black, gray or brown; underparts paler.

Species mentioned in text:
Bar-tailed godwit (*Limosa lapponica*)
Black-tailed godwit (*L. limosa*)
Common sandpiper (*Tringa hypoleucos*)
Common snipe (*Gallinago gallinago*)
Dunlin (*Calidris alpina*)
Eurasian curlew (*Numenius arquata*)
Eurasian woodcock (*Scolopax rusticola*)
Green sandpiper (*Tringa ochropus*)
Greenshank (*T. nebularia*)
Knot or Red knot (*Calidris canutus*)
Marbled godwit (*Limosa fedoa*)
Redshank (*Tringa totanus*)
Sanderling (*Calidris alba*)

sandpipers mentioned so far are all on the small side, and are often called peeps or stints.

LARGER SANDPIPERS

The larger sandpipers include snipe, woodcock, shanks, godwits and curlews. Both the Common snipe and Eurasian woodcock have a long, straight bill and mottled brown plumage. The snipe has contrasting light stripes on the back and crown. The woodcock spends most time in damp woodland, hence the name.

The shanks are noted for their long legs, red in the Redshank and green in the Greenshank. The godwits have sturdier legs and a very long bill. Both the Black-tailed and Bar-tailed godwits have a russet neck and breast in the breeding season. The Eurasian curlew has long, sturdy legs and a long, down-curved bill.

▲ **Sandpipers' bills** Little stint (*Calidris minuta*) (1), Long-billed curlew (*Numenius americanus*) (2), Curlew sandpiper (*Calidris ferruginea*) (3), Broad-billed sandpiper *(Limicola falcinellus)* (4), Spoon-billed sandpiper (*Eurynorhynchus pygmeus*) (5), turnstone (6), godwit (7), dowitcher (8), woodcock (9), snipe (10).

▼A flock of Marbled godwits on their coastal feeding grounds. They breed in north-west Canada and fly south in winter as far as Peru.

AVOCETS AND STILTS

Several pairs of avocets have come together in a rough circle on some mud flats. Each bird bends forwards and lowers the bill until it almost touches the ground. Then the birds advance in pairs, each towards another pair, doing the same thing. Occasionally as pairs press forwards, they start to scrap, but not for long. In some way this group display helps birds that nest together get rid of their desire to fight.

Avocets are among the most easily recognized of all the waders. They are handsome birds, with contrasting plumage of black and white. They have long blue-gray legs and a long dark upturned bill.

Avocets truly are waders, feeding in relatively deep water. The birds feed by sweeping the bill, partly open, from side to side in the water or soft mud. They find their prey by touch. In deep water they may reach the bottom by up-ending themselves like ducks. Also as in ducks, their feet are webbed.

AVOCETS AND STILTS Recurvirostridae
(7 species)

Habitat: fresh, brackish or salt waters.

Diet: crustaceans, worms, other invertebrates, small vertebrates.

Breeding: 2-5 (usually 4) black or brown speckled buff or greenish eggs; 22-28 days incubation.

Size: length 12-18in, weight 5-15 ounces; females usually slightly smaller.

Plumage: highly contrasting black and white patterns.

Species mentioned in text:
American avocet (*Recurvirostra americana*)
Andean avocet (*R. andina*)
Banded stilt (*Cladorhynchus leucocephalus*)
Common stilt (*Himantopus himantopus*)
Eurasian avocet (*Recurvirostra avosetta*)
Ibisbill (*Ibidorhyncha struthersii*)
Red-necked avocet (*Recurvirostra novaehollandiae*)

NOMADIC BIRDS

Four species of avocet are found in temperate and tropical regions around the world. To some extent they are nomads, moving on when their habitats change. The northern populations migrate south for the winter. The Eurasian avocet may winter as far south as the Rift Valley in East Africa. The American avocet, which is slightly bigger, breeds in western

▼The female stilt invites the male to mate by standing in shallow water in a horizontal position (1). In reply the male dips his bill in the water and shakes it and, after preening (2, 3), mounts the female (4) and mates with her (5). As he dismounts, his wing slips over his mate's back and the birds cross bills (6). The mating process usually ends with a leaning ceremony. The birds stand apart and then lean towards each other several times (7).

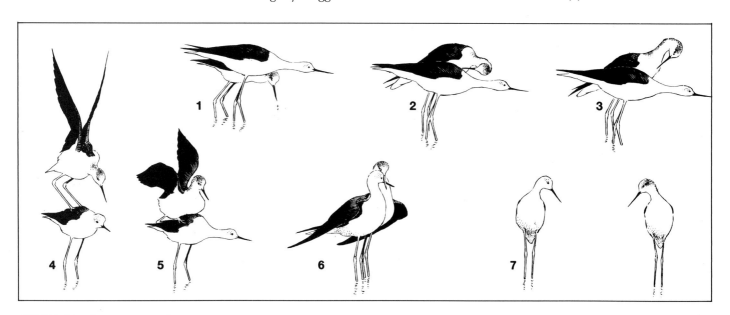

North America. It may winter as far south as Guatemala.

The main difference between the two species is that the Eurasian bird has a black cap, while the American one has a pinkish-brown neck in summer, turning white in winter. The Australasian species, the Red-necked avocet, has a sandy brown neck. The fourth species, the Andean avocet, is much darker than the others. It lives near mountain streams in the high Andes of South America.

▼ A small flock of American avocets flies in to feed, their long legs trailing behind. Note their long up-curved bills.

The ibisbill is found only in mountainous river valleys up to 14,500ft above sea level in parts of Asia.

LONG-LEGGED STILTS
The stilts are of much the same size as the avocets and are also mainly black and white. But their legs are longer and pink in color. The long bill is straight and also pink. The birds feed by stabbing at prey on or near the surface.

The Common stilt is found as slightly different races in the Old World (Europe, Asia, Africa) and the New World (the Americas). The Old World race (Black-winged stilt) lacks the black neck of the New World race (Black-necked stilt).

The New Zealand species is much darker. The Australian species, the Banded stilt, is mainly white with brown wings and has a reddish-brown band on the breast. Unlike the other stilts, it has webbed feet.

COLONIAL NESTERS
Most avocets and stilts nest in colonies. One reason they do so is because of their conspicuous plumage. Alone they would be easily spotted by predators. So they rely on the protection of the colony, as well as on their own aggressive behavior.

OYSTERCATCHERS

On the beach oystercatchers are on patrol. When birds meet their neighbors at the territorial boundaries, they launch into their noisy piping display. They strut up and down with shoulders hunched and bills pointing downwards. At the same time they utter long piping calls. These calls attract other oystercatchers, and about 30 birds gather.

Oystercatchers are wading birds that are found along the coasts in many temperate and tropical regions of the world. In places they may also be found inland around rivers and lakes, particularly in Britain, the Netherlands, Russia and New Zealand. Some species prefer rocky shorelines to sandy or muddy ones. All belong to the same genus and look and behave in much the same way.

All oystercatchers are stocky birds with a long, straight and rather blunt bill, and fairly short legs. The bill and legs are reddish-orange.

The American and Eurasian oystercatchers have a pied or black and white plumage. So has the Magellanic oystercatcher from southern South America and the Falkland Islands.

The three other members of the family are all black. They are the American Black oystercatcher (western North America), the Blackish oystercatcher (South America) and the Sooty oystercatcher (Australia).

OYSTERCATCHERS
Haematopodidae (*6 species*)

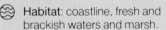 Habitat: coastline, fresh and brackish waters and marsh.

Diet: chiefly molluscs, also crabs, sea urchins, worms.

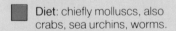 Breeding: 2-3 brown or gray, spotted and streaked eggs; 24-27 days incubation.

Size: length 15-18in; weight 15-27 ounces.

Plumage: black and white or all black.

Species mentioned in text:
American oystercatcher
(*Haematopus palliatus*)
Blackish oystercatcher (*H. ater*)
Black oystercatcher (*H. bachmani*)
Eurasian oystercatcher
(*H. ostralegus*)
Magellanic oystercatcher
(*H. leucopodus*)
Sooty oystercatcher (*H. fuliginosus*)

▼A pair of Black oystercatchers taking part in a "piping" display. These noisy displays occur when the birds become excited – for example, during courtship.

▲A Eurasian oystercatcher on its nest, a simple scrape in the ground near the sea-shore. It is lined with small pebbles and sometimes with pieces of seaweed.

MUSSELLING IN

Oystercatchers do indeed feed on oysters where they are available. But they also feed widely on mussels, cockles and clams. These molluscs are known as bivalves because they have two leaves to their shells.

If an oystercatcher comes across a mussel, say, with its shell partly open, it quickly drives in its bill. With a scissor-like action, it cuts the muscle that would spring the shell shut. Then it can remove the flesh with ease. If the shell is closed, the bird hammers into one side until it reaches the flesh. Once it has cut the muscle keeping the shell shut, it levers the two halves apart with its bill. In areas where the oystercatchers breed inland, the birds feed mainly on worms, but also on slugs and insect larvae.

FLOCKING AND NESTING

Oystercatchers are found in flocks throughout much of the year. Only when breeding do mating pairs separate and set up their own territory. Even then they still often join others for communal displays. They also help in mobbing strange birds that enter the nesting territory of their neighbors. It is during the breeding season that the piping displays become common, in the air as well as on the ground.

Oystercatchers nest in a shallow scrape on or near the sea-shore. Several scrapes may be made before the birds choose a nest site. A clutch of three eggs is usually laid. The male and female take it in turns to incubate them. Because the nest is out in the open, it is vulnerable to predators.

▲ Some scientists class these African oystercatchers as a separate species, others as a sub-species of the Eurasian oystercatcher.

When danger threatens, the parents often put on a "broken-wing" display. They run away from the nest, fluttering a wing as though they were injured. This frequently distracts the intruder and heads it in another direction. But if the eggs are taken, another clutch may be laid.

The chicks hatch fully developed and can run about almost immediately. But they cannot feed themselves because of the specialized diet of this family. The parents have to feed them, on shellfish and worms for months until they learn the techniques of shell-breaking.

GULLS

GULLS Laridae (*45 species*)

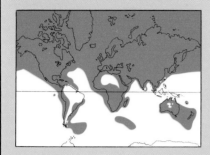

⬤ ⬛ 𝄢

〰️ Habitat: mainly coastal waters.

⬛ Diet: fish, crustaceans, molluscs, worms, carrion, eggs, chicks, refuse.

◎ Breeding: 2-3 brownish or greenish, mottled brown or gray eggs; 3-5 weeks incubation .

Size: smallest (Little gull): length 10in, weight 2lb; largest (Great black-backed gull): length up to 31in, weight 4½lb.

Plumage: white, gray and black.

Species mentioned in text:
Black-headed gull (*Larus ridibundus*)
Bonaparte's gull (*L. philadelphia*)
Common or Mew gull (*L. canus*)
Great black-backed gull (*L. marinus*)
Herring gull (*L. argentatus*)
Kittiwake or Black-legged kittiwake (*Rissa tridactyla*)
Laughing gull (*Larus atricilla*)
Lesser black-backed gull (*L. fuscus*)
Little gull (*L. minutus*)

A gull chick has decided to leave the nest and explore. It scuttles over to a nearby clump of grass, then to a pile of stones. Suddenly a piercing call rings out. Looking up, it sees an adult gull – not one of its parents – heading towards it. It has wandered into a neighbor's territory, and in a gull colony the neighbors are not friendly.

Gulls are the most common sea-birds in the Northern Hemisphere. They range widely over the northern Atlantic and Pacific and the Arctic oceans. Only a few species of gull are found south of the equator.

Gulls are very adaptable creatures and have benefited directly from the

▶**Varied plumage** The juvenile Great black- backed gull **(1)** does not have the dark wings and white underparts of the adult, nor the yellow bill. The young kittiwake **(2)** has diagonal bars on its wings and tail and neck rings, unlike the adult. The Ivory gull (*Pagophila eburnea*) **(3)** juvenile is not pure white like the adult. The young Little gull **(4)** has dark spots on its head. Sabine's gull (*Larus sabini*) **(5)** and Ross's gull (*Rhodostethia rosea*) **(6)** are both Arctic breeders. The Swallow-tailed gull (*Creagrus furcatus*) **(7)** is a tropical bird, found in the Galapagos and La Plata Islands of Ecuador.

1

activities of people. They are more and more found inland, where they scavenge for food on rubbish heaps and follow the plow on farmland. The larger species steal other birds' eggs and kill their chicks.

Gulls vary greatly in size. The Little gull is typical of the smaller gulls, with a trim body and a slender, pincer-like bill. The Great black-backed gull is a powerfully built bird with a heavy hooked bill. It looks vicious and is a fierce predator.

Most gulls have mainly white plumage underneath and pale or dark gray plumage on the back and wings. The bill and legs may be black, yellow or red. This may be a way of distinguishing gulls that otherwise look very much alike. The toes are webbed, and all the gulls are excellent swimmers. They are equally at home in the air, soaring and gliding with ease on the sea breezes.

BLACK AND WHITE HEADS

The Little gull is one of the group of hooded or masked gulls. In summer it has a black head, molting in winter to leave just dark patches. Another hooded gull in Europe is the larger Black-headed gull. This is not a good name, because in summer the head is dark brown, not black. Both birds have gray upper parts like most gulls, and the bill and legs are red. American hooded gulls include the Laughing gull and Bonaparte's gull.

The Great black-backed gull is one of the white-headed group of gulls. This group also includes the smaller Lesser black-backed gull and its close relative the Herring gull. The Herring gull is a very successful species, found throughout the north Atlantic.

The kittiwake is a much smaller white-headed bird. It spends more time at sea than most other gulls. Its name describes its strident call. The kittiwake is distinguished from the Common gull by its legs, which are black, not yellow. It catches fish by plunge-diving from the air.

SHORE, CLIFFS AND TREES
Most gulls nest in huge colonies, which they return to year after year. The nest sites are varied. The Black-headed gull nests mainly on the ground, often in a shallow scrape lined with grass and seaweed. The kittiwake favors ledges on cliffs to build its cup-shaped nest of seaweed and moss. The Herring gull nests on beach or cliff and even on roofs. Bonaparte's gull is unusual in that it nests in trees, usually conifers. The Common gull may nest in trees too, as well as on walls and buildings.

Both sexes incubate the eggs and look after the chicks when they hatch. The chicks run about as soon as their downy feathers dry. Many are killed by other gulls when their parents leave them to fish or when they wander from the nest.

▲Gray and white kittiwakes nesting in a colony on a cliff ledge below a group of black and white guillemots.

▶A Herring gull gives a loud and clear call. Its wide gape enables it to swallow large prey such as mackerel.

▼The long call of gulls (1) is a victory display. Throwing back the head (2) shows a bird is begging for food. Grass-tugging (3) takes place on the territory boundaries. Head-flagging (4) shows that the birds do not want to fight. But when they threaten each other (5), fights may break out.

TERNS

A Sandwich tern is out hunting, flying about 15ft above the waves. Soon it spots a shoal of sprats swimming near the surface. It hovers briefly before plunging into the water. Within seconds it surfaces, a wriggling sprat held in the vice-like grip of its bill. Satisfied with the kill, it flies quickly back to the nest to feed its two hungry chicks.

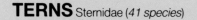

TERNS Sternidae (41 species)

● ■ 🐟

~~~ **Habitat:** mainly coastal waters, also inland waters and marshes.

■ **Diet:** fish, squid, crustaceans; marsh-dwelling species: insects, amphibians, leeches.

◎ **Breeding:** 1-3 cream, greenish or brownish, dark-blotched eggs, 18-30 days incubation.

Size: length 8-22in; weight 1¾-25 ounces.

Plumage: mainly gray, white and black.

Species mentioned in text:
Arctic tern (*Sterna paradisaea*)
Black tern (*Chlidonias nigra*)
Common tern (*Sterna hirundo*)
Inca tern (*Larosterna inca*)
Little or Least tern (*Sterna albifrons*)
Roseate tern (*S. dougallii*)
Sandwich tern (*S. sandvicensis*)
White tern (*Gygis alba*)
White-winged black tern (*Chlidonias leucoptera*)

Closely related to gulls, the terns are among the most graceful of all sea-birds. They have slender bodies, long sharply tapered wings and short legs. The head is streamlined and the bill sharply pointed.

The commonest species are the sea terns, noted for their deeply forked tail. This feature gives terns their popular name of sea swallows. The sea terns are very widely distributed, ranging from the Arctic to the Antarctic. Some species, notably the Arctic tern, migrate south thousands of miles from their nesting grounds, much of this over land.

BLACK CAPS
The sea terns include the Common, Arctic, Sandwich and Roseate terns. They all have a black cap on the head, a mainly white body and gray wings. In the Roseate tern the breast has a pinkish tinge.

The Common and Arctic terns are at first sight nearly impossible to tell

▲**Tern plumage and bill color** Blue-gray noddy (*Procelsterna cerulea*) (1), Lesser noddy (*Anous tenuirostris*) (2), White tern (3), Inca tern (4), Arctic tern (5), Long-billed tern (*Phaetusa simplex*) (6), juvenile Black tern (7), Sooty tern (*Sterna fuscata*) (8) (named after its sooty-black upperparts), Caspian tern (*S. caspia*) adult (9) and young (10).

apart. They are both the same size and have red legs. But the Common tern has its red bill tipped with black, whereas the Arctic tern's bill is red all over.

The slightly bigger Sandwich and Roseate terns can also be identified by their bills. In the first species the bill is black tipped with yellow; in the second it is black with red at the base. The Sandwich tern in addition has a short head crest.

In winter the black cap of these terns recedes slightly to give them a white forehead. A white forehead is shown in summer by the Little tern. It is the smallest of the terns with its tail

4

5

6

7

8

9

10

◄During courtship, terns perform the spectacular high-flight display (1), in which the female pursues the male to a height of several hundred feet. Later in courtship the male feeds the female (2) for some time before mating (3). After their high-flight display and mating, the birds adopt what is called the "pole stance" (4), with wings drooped and bill pointing upwards.

▼The beautiful White tern has near-transparent wings. It is found around the coasts of tropical and subtropical oceans throughout the world.

only slightly forked. It is one of the most widely distributed of the terns, found in most temperate and tropical regions except South America.

MARSH TERNS AND NODDIES

The sea terns, which belong to the genus *Sterna*, breed inland only occasionally. But species of the genus *Chlidonias* usually nest inland by rivers and lakes and in marshes. These marsh terns include the Black tern and the White-winged black tern.

In the summer the Black tern has a black head and body and smoky gray wings above and below. The White-winged black tern has a black body, but wings that are white above and black and gray below. In winter they both lose the black plumage and become very nearly indistinguishable from the sea terns. But their short tail gives them away.

In tropical regions terns known as noddies are found. They are named after their nodding displays during courtship. They have similar build to the other terns, but different plumage. Another tropical species is the Inca

tern, so named because it is native to Chile and Peru, home of the Inca civilization. Its plumage is slate colored, but its most fascinating features are the yellow mouth wattles and white moustache.

THE LONGEST MIGRATION

Of all the migrations that take place in the animal kingdom, few can rival those of the Arctic tern. The most northerly populations breed in the tundra during the short Arctic summer, then begin to fly south.

The birds that nest in the Canadian Arctic often ride the prevailing winds to western Europe. They travel south down the coast to West Africa. They may then continue down to southern Africa and from there into Antarctic waters. Or they may cross to South America and follow its coastline south to the Antarctic.

As the northern winter ends, the terns make their way back north again to their Arctic nesting sites. By the time they arrive they will have traveled up to 22,000 miles since they set out the previous year.

FAVORITE FOOD

Fish is the favorite food of sea terns. They usually catch fish by diving into the sea from the air. They swallow the fish immediately they surface, unless they are feeding young. Then they carry the catch back to the nest site.

The marsh terns eat insects, and larvae, tadpoles, spiders and leeches. They often feed on the water surface by dipping in the bill while flying. They may also dive in to catch frogs and small fish.

Noddies also dip to feed. They often catch flying fish, which are common in their tropical habitats, in mid-air. They swallow the fish and, when feeding young, regurgitate it for them at the nest.

BREEDING AND NESTING

In northern latitudes terns breed seasonally, but in the tropics they may breed at any time of the year. Most terns pair for life. Even though they wander off on their own outside the breeding season, they both return to the same nest site each year to mate.

Most sea terns breed in colonies. Their nests are usually simple scrapes in the ground, lined with a little plant material. Noddies build larger nests of vegetation in trees and bushes and on cliff ledges. Marsh terns often build floating nests anchored to the reeds. The White tern builds no nest at all, laying its single egg on a branch.

Both male and female incubate the eggs and look after the young when they hatch. In crested terns, such as the Sandwich tern, young birds often gather together for safety to form a nursery group or crèche. Parents returning with food recognize their young by voice, and feed only them.

SKUAS

A gannet is winging its way back to its rocky island nest site, belly full of fish to feed its chicks. Suddenly, out of the blue, a Great skua appears and makes straight for it. Although smaller than the gannet, the skua goes in to the attack. In panic the gannet twists and turns, but can't shake off its pursuer. Thoroughly scared and confused, the gannet brings up its last meal, which the skua immediately grabs.

SKUAS Stercorariidae
(6 species)

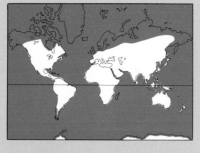

● ■

〰 Habitat: coasts, open sea.

▨ Diet: fish, krill, eggs, chicks, small mammals, insects, berries.

◯ Breeding: 2 olive, brown-marked eggs; 24-32 days (small skuas) or 45-55 days (large skuas) incubation.

Size: length 18-24in; weight 8 ounces-4lb.

Plumage: mainly brown, with pale underparts in light phase.

Species mentioned in text:
Arctic jaeger (*Stercorarius parasiticus*)
Great skua (*Catharacta skua*)
Long-tailed jaeger (*Stercorarius longicaudus*)
Pomarine jaeger (*S. pomarinus*)
South polar skua (*Catharacta maccormicki*)

▶ The Pomarine jaeger (**1**) and the Arctic jaeger (**2**), both in their light-phase plumage. The two species are much the same size and have similar markings. Besides the yellowish collar of the Pomarine, the extended tail feathers of the two birds are also different.

Skuas are powerful and aggressive birds that are the pirates of the skies. They chase and bully other birds until they disgorge (bring up) the food they have just caught. Skuas also eat the chicks and eggs of other sea-birds and small mammals.

The skuas look a lot like brown gulls. The large skuas have a heavy hooked bill and a thickset body like the big gulls. The small skuas have slighter bodies, rather like the terns. They have long feathers that project beyond the main tail plumage. All the skuas have short legs and webbed toes with sharp claws.

THE BONXIES
The Great skua is one of three species of large skuas (genus *Catharacta*) also called bonxies. They are all very similar in size and have mainly brown plumage. One population of Great

skuas breeds in the North Atlantic. Another breeds between southern South America and Antarctica.

Antarctica is also the breeding ground for the South polar skua. This bird can be found in two different forms or phases, a dark and a light. In the dark phase, it has all-over brown plumage. In the light phase, it has pale underparts.

"HUNTERS"
The three smaller skuas (genus *Stercorarius*) are also known as jaegers, from a German word for "hunter." They all breed on the Arctic tundra; and one, the Arctic jaeger, also breeds as far south as northern Britain. In winter jaegers migrate south to tropical waters and beyond.

The Arctic and Pomarine jaegers can easily be confused. Both species exist in light and dark forms. The

light-plumaged birds have pale underparts and a dark cap, with dark wings. In the dark form, the whole body is dark. In the Long-tailed jaeger, dark birds are rare. This jaeger has even longer tail feathers than the others.

CANNIBALS
Skuas usually pair for life. They may build their nests in loose colonies, as in the Shetland Isles. Or they may nest separately, as on the Arctic tundra. The nests are usually simple scrapes in the ground, sparsely lined with grass or moss. Both sexes share the incubation of the eggs and later the feeding of the chicks. Usually two chicks are raised. But if food is scarce the first chick to hatch will kill the second, or the parents will.

▼The Great skua is a powerful bird that will attack birds bigger than itself. It will also dive-bomb intruders near its nest.

SKIMMERS

It is very nearly dark over the inland Salton Sea in California, yet some birds are still active. They are flying low over the water with their wingtips nearly touching the surface. The body is angled forwards so that the lower part of the open bill dips into the water. They are Black skimmers going fishing. Here and there a bird strikes lucky as the lower bill touches a fish. It snaps the head down and closes the bill over the fish. Then it lifts the head up and swallows its catch.

Skimmers are named after the way they skim over the surface when feeding. They have an extraordinary bill, with the lower mandible much longer than the upper one. Both mandibles are flat, like the blades of a pair of scissors. This gives the birds their popular name of scissorbill.

The muscles and bones in the head of the bird are specially adapted to the method of feeding. They act as a shock absorber when the head snaps down and the bill shuts as prey is caught.

Skimmers usually fish either alone or in pairs, only occasionally in small groups. They mostly feed at dusk and often during the night. Unusually, their eyes have a vertical slit pupil, like a cat's eye. This may help them see better in the dark.

CLOSE RELATIONS

The three species of skimmer are found mainly in tropical and subtropical regions of the world. They are of similar size and appearance.

Apart from the bill, skimmers resemble the sea terns. They have an elegant body, short legs and a black cap and nape. Their wings are very long and sharply tapered, with a span 2½ times their body length. The wings and back are dark, the underparts white or pale gray. The main differences between the species are in the color of the bill and legs.

The Black skimmer represents the skimmers in the New World. It has bright red legs and an orange bill tipped with black. It breeds in the United States and in Central and South America. The slightly smaller Indian skimmer is similar except for an all-orange bill. It ranges from Pakistan, through India to the Malay peninsula. The African skimmer, of Central and East Africa, has yellowish legs and a yellowish-orange bill.

In the United States, the Black skimmer is a bird of the coasts and the inland Salton Sea. In South America it inhabits the river systems. The Indian and African skimmers are also found mainly along inland waterways.

BELLY WETTING

Skimmers nest in colonies, typically in the open on sand bars in rivers and estuaries. They sometimes nest alongside terns. This probably helps protect

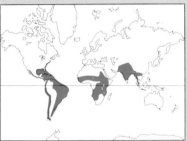

SKIMMERS Rynchopidae
(3 species)

● ■

~ Habitat: coastal and inland waters, marshes.

■ Diet: small fish, shrimps, other crustaceans.

○ Breeding: 2-5 white to brownish, dark-blotched or spotted eggs; 22-24 days incubation.

Size: length 14-18in; weight up to 14 ounces.

Plumage: upper parts dark, underparts pale.

Species mentioned in text:
African skimmer (*Rynchops flavirostris*)
Black skimmer (*R. niger*)
Indian skimmer (*R. albicollis*)

▼ The Black skimmer of the Americas is the largest member of the family. But all skimmers have this odd-looking bill.

them better against predators, because the terns are more aggressive against intruders.

Before mating and nesting, skimmers become very active and noisy, especially at night. Their courtship displays include vigorous high-speed aerial chases. Skimmers make their nests in shallow hollows in the sand which they excavate with the breast.

▼A Black skimmer foraging for food. The bill snaps shut instantly when the long lower part touches a fish.

Both males and females incubate the eggs. At tropical nest sites in particular, the birds swap duty frequently during the day when the temperature of the sand soars. Before relieving its mate, each bird dips its belly and feet in the water. When back on the nest, this wets the eggs and helps prevent them from becoming overheated.

The parents feed the young with small fish. The young can pick them up because to begin with the two mandibles of the bill are the same size.

They also feed themselves on insects at this time. Only when the young start to fly does the bottom mandible begin to lengthen. Then the birds fly with their parents on fishing trips and learn to skim for themselves.

Although a nesting pair can successfully raise as many as four young, most pairs do not do so. On the open low-lying nest sites, the eggs are often washed away by high tides or flooding. Snakes, lizards and herons may prey on the eggs too and also on newly hatched chicks.

AUKS

The razorbill chicks are about three weeks old. Under the watchful eyes of their fathers, they gather on the cliff ledge, high above the sea. They are not yet fully grown and cannot fly. As time goes by they get more and more excited, jumping up and down and flapping their tiny wings. Then one by one they launch themselves into the air. They flutter helplessly down into the sea arriving shaken, but otherwise none the worse for wear.

The auk family includes some of our best-known and oddest-looking sea-birds, including puffins, guillemots, and razorbills. All the auks are expert swimmers and divers, and they feed underwater.

In many ways auks can be considered the penguins of the Northern Hemisphere. Their short, strong legs and webbed feet are set well back on the body. When they stand, the body is upright. When they swim underwater, they use their wings and feet for propulsion and steering. But they differ from penguins in one important respect – they can fly.

Some of the auks have alternative names. The Common guillemot is often called the murre. The Black guillemot is sometimes called the tystie; the Little auk, the dovekie. The

▼Razorbills nesting on a cliff ledge. These stocky, thick-necked birds are well named for their bill is razor sharp and a formidable weapon.

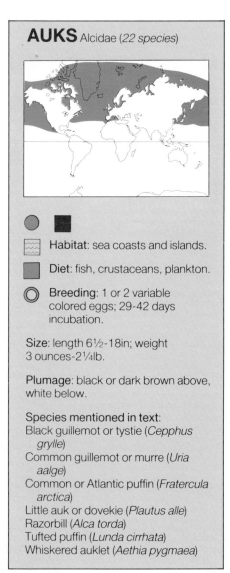

AUKS Alcidae (*22 species*)

⬤ ■

〰 Habitat: sea coasts and islands.

■ Diet: fish, crustaceans, plankton.

◎ Breeding: 1 or 2 variable colored eggs; 29-42 days incubation.

Size: length 6½-18in; weight 3 ounces-2¼lb.

Plumage: black or dark brown above, white below.

Species mentioned in text:
Black guillemot or tystie (*Cepphus grylle*)
Common guillemot or murre (*Uria aalge*)
Common or Atlantic puffin (*Fratercula arctica*)
Little auk or dovekie (*Plautus alle*)
Razorbill (*Alca torda*)
Tufted puffin (*Lunda cirrhata*)
Whiskered auklet (*Aethia pygmaea*)

1

2

3

4

Little auk is well named because at 8in long it is only half the size of the Common guillemot, the biggest auk. Other small auks include the auklets and the murrelets, popularly called sea sparrows.

IN TWO OCEANS
The Common and Black guillemots breed in the North Atlantic and

▼In its colorful bill, the Common puffin can catch several fish during each dive.

around the Bering Strait. They nest in the far north, then swim south to warmer waters.

The razorbill and Common or Atlantic puffin breed only in the North Atlantic. They both have a distinctive chunky bill. The puffin's is triangular and highly colored. In addition to the usual black above and white below plumage of most auks, the puffin has white face patches. Its short thick legs and feet are red. All this adds up to a rather clown-like appearance.

▲Common guillemots nest very close together in dense colonies. Even so, they each occupy and protect a small territory. When a neighbor comes too close, the guillemot puts on a threat display (1). Fighting may break out, but is soon over when one of the birds begins to side-preen (2) or stretch or turn away (3). In another appeasement (giving-in) display (4), a bird walks in a ritual way through another's territory.

There are puffin species in the Pacific as well, including the Tufted puffin. This has dark underparts and magnificent head plumes during the breeding season. Other tufted Pacific residents include several species of auklet, including the Whiskered auklet. These small birds, like the Little auk of the Atlantic, feed mainly on plankton.

TOGETHERNESS
Auks mostly breed in colonies, and several species often nest together. The Common guillemot breeds more closely together than any other bird species. This often leads to squabbles, but these birds have many different calls and displays to help them communicate and live in harmony.

The Common guillemot and the razorbill lay their eggs on bare cliff ledges, the Black guillemot in crevices. Puffins and auklets nest in burrows they hollow out of the ground.

Most auk young remain at the nest site until they are almost full-grown and ready to fly out to sea. Razorbill young tumble into the sea much earlier and mature there, looked after by their fathers. Young murrelets go to sea when they are only 2 days old!

▲ The Tufted puffin grows short hairs on its face in the breeding season and, like other auks, has a summer plumage with more white feathers.

► Common guillemots crowd together in their thousands on the ledges of their cliff colony. Up to 70 pairs per sq yd have been recorded! Communal nesting like this helps keep away predators, such as gulls and crows. But it also results in eggs being knocked off the cliff-face.

▼ The Black guillemot is unmistakable in its summer plumage. It is all black, except for white patches on the wings. The legs and mouth are bright red.

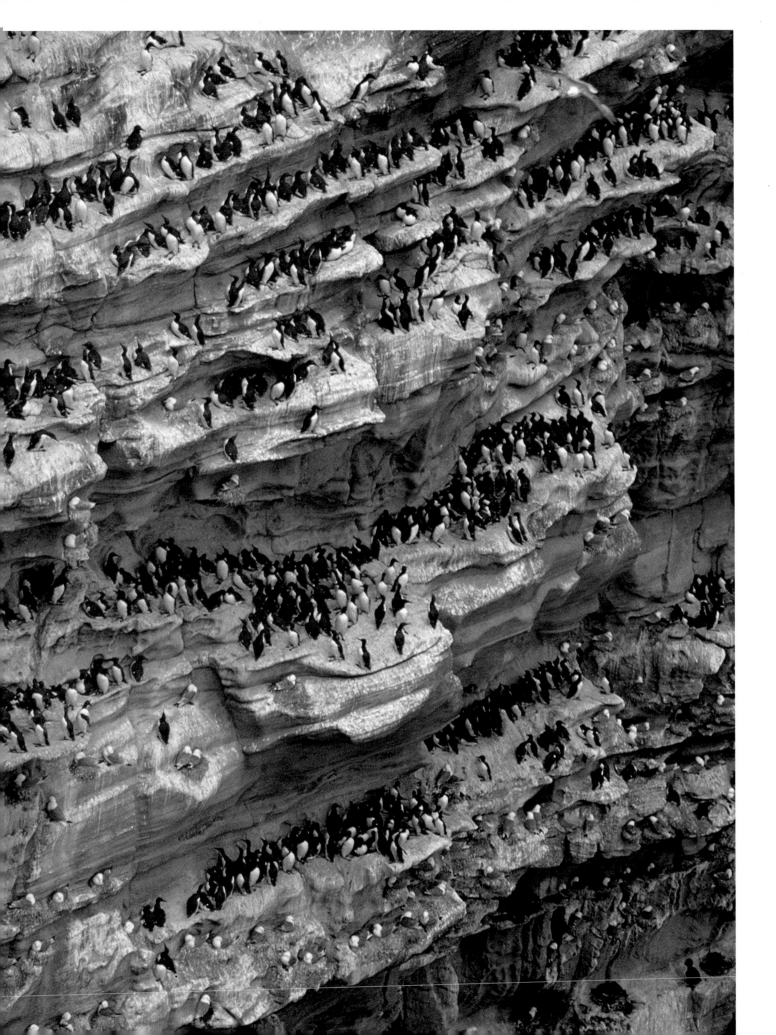

GLOSSARY

Adaptation Any feature of an animal's body or life-style that suits it to live in its surroundings.

Aggression Any behavior in which one animal threatens another.

Air sacs Little air-filled bags in a bird's body connected to its lungs which help increase the amount of air a bird breathes in.

Antarctic The bitterly cold region in the far south of the world, around the South Pole.

Aquatic Living for much, if not all, of the time in the water.

Arctic The bitterly cold region in the far north of the world, around the North Pole within the Arctic Circle.

Aves The class of animals to which all birds belong.

Avian Relating to birds.

Bill Also called beak; the horny part of a bird's mouth with which it gathers food.

Brood The group of young raised in a single breeding cycle.

Call The sounds a bird makes.

Camouflage Color and patterns on an animal's coat that allow it to blend in with its surroundings.

Carrion Meat from a dead animal.

Class The division of animal classi-fication above Order. All birds belong to the class Aves.

Clutch The eggs a bird lays in one breeding session.

Colonial Living, especially breeding, in colonies.

Competition The contest between two or more species over such things as space and food.

Coniferous forest Forest of trees with needle-like leaves, which usually bear leaves all year.

Conservation Preserving and protecting living things, their habitat and the environment in general.

Crèche A gathering of young birds, usually for protection.

Crest On a bird, a set of long feathers on the top of the head.

Crustaceans Shelled creatures, like crabs, shrimps, krill and copepods.

Deciduous forest Forest of trees that shed their leaves seasonally, usually in winter.

Diet The food an animal eats.

Display A typical pattern of behavior associated with important aspects of an animal's life, such as courtship, mating, nesting and defending territory.

Disruptive plumage Plumage so patterned and colored that it breaks up a bird's outline and enables it to camouflage itself in its natural habitat.

Diurnal Active during the day.

Eclipse plumage The plumage of male ducks after breeding, in which they lose their bright feathers and for a short while look like the females.

Endangered species One whose numbers have dropped so low that it is in danger of becoming extinct.

Environment The surroundings of a particular species, or the world about us in general.

Estuary The broad mouth of a river when it meets the sea. Estuaries are important feeding grounds for most waders, especially in the winter.

Eurasia The great land mass of Europe and Asia.

Extinction The complete loss of a species, either locally or on the Earth.

Family The division of animal classification below Order and above Genus. In the bird world there are 163 recognized families.

Fledging The time when a young bird first takes to the air; a fledgling is a bird that has just begun to fly.

Flight feathers The large feathers on the wings, which are divided into the primaries and secondaries.

Foraging Going in search of food.

Frontal shield A bare fleshy area covering a bird's forehead.

Genus The division of animal classification below Family and above Species. In the bird world there are 1,975 recognized genera.

Gregarious Liking to be with others of their kind. Most sea-birds and waders are gregarious.

Guano The accumulated waste (excreta) of birds, exploited in some parts of the world as fertilizer.

Habitat The type of surroundings in which an animal lives.

Hatching The moment when a young bird emerges from the egg; hence hatchling, a young bird that has recently hatched.

Home range The area in which an animal usually lives and feeds.

Incubation The period during which a bird sits on a clutch of eggs to keep them warm so that they will develop and eventually hatch.

Invertebrates Animals without backbones, such as insects and worms. They are a source of food for many birds.

Krill Shrimp-like creatures that are eaten by some birds.

Mammals Animals whose females have mammary glands, which produce milk on which they feed their young. Small mammals are food for some birds.

Marine Living in or on the sea and, in the case of birds, on the shore.

Migration The long-distance movement of animals. It is typically seasonal, e.g. between far northern breeding grounds in summer and warmer southern regions in winter.

Milk A fluid produced in the crop of pigeons (and flamingos), which the birds use to feed their newly hatched young. It has much the same food value as mammal milk.

Molt The period when a bird sheds old feathers and grows new ones.

Nestling A young bird in the nest.

Nocturnal Active during the night.

Omnivore An animal with a varied diet, eating both plants and animals.

Order The division of animal classification below Class and above Family. There are 28 recognized orders in the bird world.

Plumage The feathers of a bird. Many birds have a different plumage in the spring and summer breeding season from that in the winter. The breeding plumage is often vivid, the winter plumage dull.

Population A separate group of birds of the same species.

Predator An animal that hunts and kills other animals, its prey.

Preening Running the bill through the feathers to keep the plumage clean and airworthy. The action also distributes oil onto the plumage from a preen gland just above the tail.

Primaries The long outer flight feathers on the wings, with which a bird propels itself through the air.

Race The division of animal classification below Sub-species; it refers to animals that are very similar but have slightly different characteristics.

Regurgitate Bring up food previously swallowed. Many sea-birds feed their young by regurgitation.

Resident An animal that stays in the same area all year round.

Roosting Sleeping or resting.

Savannah Tropical grassland, particularly in Africa.

Scrape A hollow in the ground made by an animal in which it lays its eggs.

Secondaries The shorter inner flight feathers on the wing that provide the lift that keeps a bird in the air.

Solitary Living alone for most of the time.

Species The division of animal classification below Genus; a group of animals of the same structure which can breed with one another.

Sub-species The division of animal classification below Species and above Race; typically the sub-species are separated into different places.

Temperate A climate that is not too hot and not too cold. Temperate zones lie between the sub-tropics and the cold high-latitude regions in both hemispheres.

Territory The area in which an animal or group of animals lives and defends against intruders.

Tropics Strictly, the region between latitudes 23° north and south of the equator. Tropical regions are typically very hot and humid.

Tundra The landscape at high latitudes where the very cold climate prevents the growth of trees. A similar habitat occurs at high altitudes on mountains.

Vertebrates Animals with backbones. Birds are terrestrial vertebrates.

Waders Birds of the seashore and marsh that feed in the shallows. Large waders include the lapwing, avocet, oystercatcher, godwit and curlew. Small waders include knot, dunlin, common sandpiper, redshank and snipe. They all belong to the order Charadriiformes.

Waterfowl Birds such as swans, geese and ducks, belonging to the order Anseriformes.

Wattles Fleshy growths on the head of some birds, usually near the base of the bill. They may be highly colored.

Wintering ground The region where migrant birds go to outside the breeding season; usually in warmer lower latitudes.

INDEX

Common names

Single page numbers indicate a major section of the main text. Double, hyphenated, numbers refer to major articles. **Bold numbers** refer to illustrations.

albatross
  Black-browed **19**
  Black-footed 18
  Laysan **18**
  Light-mantled sooty 19
  Royal 18
  Sooty 18
  Wandering 18, **19**
  Waved 18
albatrosses 18-19
  great 18
  sooty 18
  see also albatross,
    mollymawks
auk
  Little 86, 87, 88
auklet
  Whiskered 88
auklets 87, 88
  see also auklet
auks 86-89
  see also auk, auklets,
    guillemots, murrelets,
    puffins, razorbills
avocet
  American 70, **71**
  Andean 71
  Eurasian 70, 71
  Red-necked 71
avocets 70-71
  see also avocet

bittern
  Least 38
bitterns 36-39
  true 38
  see also bittern
bonxies *see* skuas
boobies 26-29
  see also booby
booby
  Abbott's **26**, 28, 29
  Blue-footed **28**
  Brown 27, **28**
  Masked *see* booby, White
  Peruvian **26**, 28, 29
  Red-footed **27**, 28
  White **26**, 27, 28

coot
  American 62
  Crested 63
  European **62**
  Giant 62
  Horned 63
coots 62
  see also coot
cormorant
  Black *see* cormorant,
    Common
  Common 32

Galapagos flightless **33**
Great *see* cormorant,
  Common
Peru *see* guanay
Reed **32**
cormorants 32-33
  see also cormorant
corncrake 63
crake
  Black **63**
  Spotted 63
crakes 62, 63
  see also crake
crane
  Black-crowned **60**
  Blue 58, **59**
  Common 58
  Demoiselle **58**, 59
  Siberian 58
  Stanley *see* crane, Blue
  Whooping 58, 60
cranes 58-61
  see also crane, limpkin
curlew
  Eurasian 69
  Long-billed **69**
curlews 69
  see also curlew

dabchick *see* grebe, Little
darter
  African **33**
  darters 32-33
  see also darter
divers *see* loons
dovekie *see* auk, Little
dowitcher **69**
duck
  Black-headed **55**
  Freckled 54
  Mandarin **54**, 57
  North American wood 57
  Ruddy **54**, 56
  Tufted **54**, **56**
  White-faced tree **54**
ducks 7, 54-57
  bay *see* ducks, diving
  dabbling 54, 55
  diving 54, 56, 57
  perching 54, 57
  sea 54, 57
  steamer 54, 57
  tree *see* ducks, whistling
  whistling 54, 57
  see also duck, eider,
    goosander, mallard,
    mergansers, pintail,
    pochard, redhead,
    sawbills, scaups, scoter,
    shelduck, shoveler,
    stifftails, teal
dunlin 68

egret
  Cattle 37
  Common *see* heron, Great
    white
  Great white *see* heron,
    Great white

eider
  Common **56**, 57

flamingo
  Andean 45
  Caribbean **44**, 45
  Chilean **44**, **46**
  Greater **44**, **45**, **46**
  James's 45
  Lesser 44, 45, **46**
flamingos 7, 44-47
  see also flamingo
frigatebird
  Andrew's 34
  Ascension Island 34
  Christmas Island *see*
    frigatebird, Andrew's
  Great **34**
  Lesser 34, **35**
  Magnificent **34**
frigatebirds 34-35
  see also frigatebird
fulmar
  Northern 20
  Southern 20
fulmars 20-21
  see also fulmar

gallinule
  Common *see* moorhen
  Purple **63**
gallinules 62, 63
  see also gallinule
gannet
  African *see* gannet, Cape
  Atlantic **26**, 27
  Australasian **26**, 27
  Cape **27**, 28
gannets 26-29
  see also gannet
geese 48-53
  black 50
  perching 54
  see also goose
godwit **69**
  Bar-tailed 69
  Black-tailed 69
  Marbled **69**
godwits 69
  see also godwit
goosander 54, 57
goose
  Bar-headed **50**
  Barnacle 50
  Canada **49**, 50
  Emperor **50**, 52
  Hawaiian **50**
  Magpie **50**, 52
  Pink-footed **50**, 52
  Red-breasted **50**
  Snow **48**, 52
grebe
  Atitlan 17
  Black-necked **17**
  Great-crested **16**, **17**
  Horned *see* grebe,
    Slavonian
  Little 16, **17**
  Pied-billed 16, **17**

Red-necked **17**
Slavonian 16, **17**
Swan *see* grebe, Western
Western 16, **17**
grebes 7, 16-17
  see also grebe
greenshank 69
guanay 32
guillemot
  Black 86, 87, **88**
  Common 86, **87**, **88**
guillemots 86
  see also guillemot
gull
  Black-headed 75, 76
  Bonaparte's 75, 76
  Common 76
  Great black-backed **74**, 75
  Herring 75, **76**
  Ivory **74**
  Laughing 75
  Lesser black-backed 75
  Little **74**, 75
  Mew *see* gull, Common
  Ross's **74**
  Sabine's **74**
  Swallow-tailed **74**
gulls **7**, 74-77
  hooded 75
  masked *see* gulls, hooded
  white-headed 75
  see also gull, kittiwake

hammerhead 40
heron
  Black-crowned night 38
  Black **37**
  Gray 36, **37**, **38**
  Great blue 37
  Great White **36**, 37
  Lined **36**
  Purple **36**
  Tiger *see* heron, Lined
  Yellow-crowned night **36**
herons 36-39
  day 37
  night 38
  tiger 38
  see also egret, heron
hummingbird
  Bee 9
  Vervain 9

ibis
  American white **42**, **43**
  Bald 42, 43
  Glossy **42**
  Japanese **42**
  Sacred 42
  Scarlet **42**, **43**
ibisbill 71
ibises 42-43
  see also ibis

jaeger
  Long-tailed 83
  Parasitic **82**, 83
  Pomarine **82**, 83
jaegers *see* jaeger

Scientific names

The first name of each double-barrel Latin name refers to the *Genus*, the second to the *species*. Single names not in *italic* refer to a family or sub-family and are cross-referenced to the Common name index.

Aechmorphorus occidentalis (Western grebe) 16, 17
Aethia pygmaea (Whiskered auklet) 88
Aix
   galericulata (Mandarin duck) 54, 57
   sponsa (North American wood duck) 57
Alca torda (razorbill) 86, 87, 88
Alcidae *see* auks
Anarhynchus frontalis (wrybill) 64
Anas
   acuta (pintail) 55, 56
   clypeata (shoveler) 55, 56
   crecca (teal) 55
   platyrhynchos (mallard) 55, 56
Anastomus lamelligerus (African open-bill stork) 41
Anatidae *see* ducks, swans and geese
Anhimidae *see* swans and geese
Anhinga rufa (African darter) 33
anhingas *see* darters
Anhingidae *see* cormorants
Anous tenuirostris (Lesser noddy) 78
Anser
   brachyrhyncus (Pink-footed goose) 50, 52
   caerulescens (Snow goose) 48, 52
   canagicus (Emperor goose) 50, 52
   indicus (Bar-headed goose) 50
Anseranas semipalmata (Magpie goose) 50, 52
Anthropoides
   paradisea (Blue or Stanley crane) 58, 59
   virgo (Demoiselle crane) 58, 59
Aptenodytes
   forsteri (Emperor penguin) 10, 13
   patagonicus (King penguin) 10, 13
Aramidae *see* cranes
Aramus guarauna (limpkin) 58
Ardea
   cinerea (Gray heron) 36, 37, 38
   herodius (Great blue heron) 37
   purpurea (Purple heron) 36

Ardeinae *see* herons and bitterns
Aythya
   americana (redhead) 56
   ferina (Common or European pochard) 56
   fuligula (Tufted duck) 54, 56

Balaeniceps rex (Whale-headed stork) 40
Balaenicipitidae *see* storks
Balearica pavonina (Black-crowned crane) 60
Botaurinae *see* herons and bitterns
Branta
   canadiensis (Canada goose) 49, 50
   leucopsis (Barnacle goose) 50
   ruficollis (Red-breasted goose) 50
   sandvicensis (Hawaiian goose) 50
Bubulcus ibis (Cattle egret) 37
Bugeranus leucogeranus (Siberian crane) 58

Calidris
   alba (sanderling) 68
   alpina (dunlin) 68
   canutus (knot or Red knot) 68
   ferruginea (Curlew sandpiper) 69
   minuta (Little stint) 69
Catharacta
   maccormicki (South polar skua) 83
   skua (Great skua) 82, 83
Cepphus grylle (Black guillemot or tystie) 86, 87, 88
Charadriidae *see* plovers
Charadrius
   dubius (Little ringed plover) 64, 65
   hiaticula (Ringed plover) 64, 65
   melanops (Black-fronted plover) 64
   vociferus (killdeer) 65
Chauna torquata (Crested screamer) 50
Chlidonias
   leucoptera (White-winged black tern) 80
   nigra (Black tern) 78, 80
Ciconia
   ciconia (White stork) 40, 41
   nigra (Black stork) 40, 41
Ciconiidae *see* storks
Cladorhynchus
   leucocephalus (Banded stilt) 71
Creagrus furcatus (Swallow-tailed gull) 74
Crex crex (corncrake) 63
Cygnus
   atrata (Black swan) 49, 50
   buccinator (Trumpeter swan) 50

   columbianus (Bewick's or Whistling swan) 49
   cygnus (Whooper swan) 49, 50
   melanchoryphus (Black-necked swan) 50
   olor (Mute swan) 48, 49, 50, 52
Dendrocygna viduata (White-faced tree duck) 54
Diomedea
   epomophora (Royal albatross) 18
   exulans (Wandering albatross) 18, 19
   immutabilis (Laysan albatross) 18
   irrorata (Waved albatross) 18
   melanophris (Black-browed albatross) 19
   nigripes (Black-footed albatross) 18
Diomedeidae *see* albatrosses

Egretta
   alba (Great white heron) 36, 37
   ardesiaca (Black heron) 37
Eudocimus
   albus (American white ibis) 42, 43
   ruber (Scarlet ibis) 42, 43
Eudyptes crestatus (Rockhopper penguin) 10, 11
Eurynorhynchus pygmeus (Spoon-billed sandpiper) 69

Fratercula arctica (Common or Atlantic puffin) 87
Fregata
   andrewsi (Andrew's or Christmas Island frigatebird) 34
   aquila (Ascension Island frigatebird) 34
   ariel (Lesser frigatebird) 34, 35
   magnificens (Magnificent frigatebird) 34
   minor (Great frigatebird) 34
Fregatidae *see* frigatebirds
Fulica
   americana (American coot) 62
   atra (European coot) 62
   cornuta (Horned coot) 63
   cristata (Crested coot) 63
   gigantea (Giant coot) 62
Fulmarus glacialis (Northern and Southern fulmars) 20

Gallinago gallinago (Common snipe) 68, 69
Gallinula chloropus (moorhen or Common gallinule) 63
Garrodia nereis (Gray-backed storm petrel) 21
Gavia
   adamsii (Yellow-billed loon) 14

   arctica (Arctic loon) 14, 15
   immer (Common loon) 14, 15
   stellata (Red-throated loon) 14
Gaviidae *see* divers
Geronticus calvus (Bald ibis) 42, 43
Gruidae *see* cranes
Grus 60
   americana (Whooping crane) 58, 60
   grus (Common crane) 58
Gygis alba (White tern) 78, 80, 81

Haematopodidae *see* oystercatchers
Haematopus
   ater (Blackish oystercatcher) 72
   bachmani (Black oystercatcher) 72
   fuliginosus (Sooty oystercatcher) 72
   leucopodus (Magellanic oystercatcher) 72
   ostralegus (Eurasian oystercatcher) 72, 73
   palliatus (American oystercatcher) 72
Heteronetta atricapilla (Black-headed duck) 55
Himantopus himantopus (Common stilt) 71
Hydrobatidae *see* shearwaters

Ibidorhyncha struthersii (ibisbill) 71
Ibis ibis (Yellow-billed stork) 41
Ixobrychus exilis (Least bittern) 38

Laridae *see* gulls
Larosterna inca (Inca tern) 78, 80
Larus
   argentatus (Herring gull) 75, 76
   atricilla (Laughing gull) 75
   canus (Common or Mew gull) 76
   fuscus (Lesser black-backed gull) 75
   marinus (Great black-backed gull) 74, 75
   minutus (Little gull) 74, 75
   philadelphia (Bonaparte's gull) 75, 76
   ridibundus (Black-headed gull) 75, 76
   sabini (Sabine's gull) 74
Leptoptilos crumeniferus (marabou) 40
Limicola falcinellus (Broad-billed sandpiper) 69
Limnocorax flavirostra (Black crake) 63
Limosa
   fedoa (Marbled godwit) 69